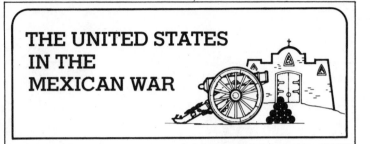

THE UNITED STATES
IN THE
MEXICAN WAR

THE
UNITED STATES
IN THE
MEXICAN WAR

Don Lawson

*Illustrated with photographs, and maps and
drawings by Robert F. McCullough*

ABELARD-SCHUMAN
New York

Library of Congress Cataloging in Publication Data
Lawson, Don.
    The United States in the Mexican War.
    (The Young people's history of America's wars series)
    Bibliography: p.   Includes index.
    SUMMARY: A detailed account of the events leading up
to and through the war which the United States fought
against Mexico.
    1. United States—History—War with Mexico, 1845–1848
—Campaigns and battles—Juv. lit. 2. Alamo—Siege, 1836
—Juvenile literature. 3. Texas—History—Republic, 1836–
1846—Juv. lit. [1. United States—History—War with Mexico, 1845–1848—Campaigns and battles. 2. Alamo—Siege,
1836. 3. Texas—History—Republic, 1836–1846] I. McCullough, Robert F., 1929–   II. Title.
E405.L38   1976   973.6′2   76-11022
ISBN 0-200-00169-8
10 9 8 7 6 5 4 3 2

To Frances Schwartz
with affection and
admiration

Books by DON LAWSON

Contents

Illustrations

MAPS

PHOTOGRAPHS

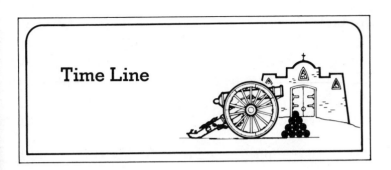

Time Line

1836

Siege of the Alamo ends in Mexican victory, March 6.
Sam Houston and Texans defeat Santa Anna at Battle
of San Jacinto, April 21; Texas gains independence.

1845

Polk inaugurated as U.S. president, March 4.
United States annexes Texas, December 29.

1846

Taylor wins battles of Palo Alto and Resaca de la
Palma before war officially begins, May 8 and 9.
United States declares war on Mexico, May 13.
Kearny begins march to New Mexico and west coast,
June 5.

Santa Anna returns to Mexico from exile in Havana, Cuba, August 16.

Kearny reaches Santa Fe, August 18.

Taylor wins Battle of Monterrey, Mexico, September 20–24.

Scott named to lead Veracruz–Mexico City campaign, November 18.

March of Doniphan's Thousand begins, December 12.

1847

Stockton takes over Los Angeles, January 10.

Taylor wins Battle of Buena Vista, February 22–23.

Doniphan takes over Chihuahua, March 1.

First major amphibious landing in history by U.S. troops at Veracruz, March 9.

Veracruz surrenders to Scott, March 29.

Scott begins march to Mexico City, April 8.

Trist named peace commissioner by President Polk, April 15.

Scott wins Battle of Cerro Gordo, April 18.

Puebla occupied by U.S. forces, May 15.

Scott wins battles of Contreras and Churubusco, August 19–20.

Battle of the King's Mill won by Scott, September 8.

Scott wins Battle of Chapultepec, September 13.

Mexico City occupied by Scott, September 14.

Santa Anna resigns as president of Mexico, September 16.

Polk recalls Trist, October 6; Trist receives orders six weeks later, decides to stay on in Mexico to seek peace.

1848

Scott recalled and replaced as commanding general by President Polk; General William O. Butler named as Scott's replacement, January 13.

Treaty of Guadalupe Hidalgo signed, February 2; ratified by U.S. Senate on March 10, and by Mexican government officials on March 25.

American troops leave Mexico City, June 12.

Last troopships sail from Veracruz, August 1.

1
"Remember the Alamo!"

To the people of Texas and all Americans in the world—Fellow citizens—& compatriots—I am besieged by a thousand or more of the Mexicans under Santa Anna. I have sustained a continual bombardment and cannonade for 24 hours & have not lost a man. The enemy has demanded a surrender at discretion, otherwise the garrison are to be put to the sword if the fort is taken. I have answered the demand with a cannon shot, and our flag still waves proudly from the walls. I shall never surrender or retreat. *Then, I call on you in the name of Liberty, of patriotism & everything dear to the American character, to come to our aid with all dispatch. The enemy is receiving reinforcement daily & will no doubt increase to three or four thousand in four or five days. If this call is neglected, I am determined to sustain myself as long as possible & die like a soldier who never forgets what is due to his own honor & that of his country.* Victory or Death!

1

These were the heroic words that announced the opening of the siege of a fortified mission called the Alamo at San Antonio, Texas. The siege was one of the epic battles in American history. The words were written by the fort's commander, Lieutenant Colonel William Barret Travis, on February 24, 1836. Travis's combat command numbered about 150 Americans. Surrounding them outside the Alamo's walls were 3,000 Mexicans led by Mexico's top general, the fiery and ruthless Antonio López de Santa Anna.

Although the whole of Texas and much of the rest of the United States were alerted by Travis's plea for help, time proved too short to allow any large number of reinforcements to reach the besieged fortress. A small band of 32 brave men and boys did manage to make their way from nearby Gonzales, through the Mexican lines, but no further aid arrived. Nevertheless, Travis and his men stubbornly held out against the constant bombardment.

Included among the staunch patriots defending the Alamo were several legendary frontier fighters. One was Colonel James Bowie, who had made famous the bowie knife—an eight-inch-long, single-edged blade, an inch and a quarter wide. The knife was originally designed by Jim Bowie's older brother, Rezin Pleasants' Bowie, as a hunting weapon. Jim, however, had not hesitated to use it in occasional hand-to-hand combat, and he was prepared to do so now if the Mexicans stormed their way into the fort.

William Barret Travis

3

James Bowie
PHOTO: SAN JACINTO MUSEUM OF HISTORY

But Jim Bowie would have to defend himself, not standing on his own two legs, but flat on his back on a hospital cot. Shortly after his arrival at the Alamo, just a few weeks earlier, Bowie had fallen ill with pneumonia and was soon unable to stand.

Also among the famed Alamo defenders were the frontiersman Davy Crockett and his "Tennessee Boys." In a sense they were "volunteer Texas patriots," who had made their way from their native Tennessee when they learned that the cause of American freedom was being threatened on the Texas frontier.

Davy Crockett was already an American legend before he took part in the heroic last stand at the Alamo. A native of Tennessee, he had been an expert marksman and woodsman from boyhood. One year, while still in his teens, he killed more than a hundred bears. Crockett was also extremely popular as a young man. He had been elected twice to the state legislature and three times to the U.S. House of Representatives. In 1835, however, he had been defeated for reelection to Congress. His reaction to this defeat was to put on his coonskin cap, pick up his rifle, "Old Betsy," and tell his neighbors: "You-all can go to hell, and I'm goin' t' Texas!"

To Texas he and a number of his loyal followers went, and now they found themselves about to take part in the last act of a dramatic fight for their very lives.

Also among those inside the Alamo were several

civilian families and their servants. Included among the civilians were the wife, Susanna, and baby daughter, Angelina, of one of the officers, Captain Almeron Dickinson.

The bombardment continued relentlessly for ten days. In the midst of the constant shelling, Colonel Travis made no attempt to disguise the hopelessness of the situation to his men. Nevertheless, he demanded, and got, their complete loyalty. During one brief lull, he assembled his command in the courtyard and issued his final commands. Then, unsheathing his sword, he used it to draw a line in the dust.

"Those prepared to give their lives in freedom's cause," Colonel Travis said, "step across that line toward me."

Colonel Jim Bowie demanded that his cot be carried across the line. All of the rest of the men, except one, also crossed Travis's mark in the dust. The one man who decided to try to escape from the Alamo, rather than remain and face certain death, was Louis Moses Rose, a middle-aged veteran of the Napoleonic wars in Europe. Both Bowie and Crockett tried to persuade him to cross Travis's line and join them in their last battle, but Rose refused. He decided he had seen enough of death and destruction. That night he made his way over the Alamo wall and disappeared toward the Mexican lines. Somehow he managed to make good his escape, but he kept his identity a secret until many years later, when he identified himself to a family in east

Texas and told them of Colonel Travis's final challenge to his men and how heroically all of them, except himself, had responded. (Many legends grew out of the defense of the Alamo, and the story about Rose may be one of them. Some historians even claim that Davy Crockett survived the massacre, but there is no convincing proof of this. Actually, Mrs. Dickinson, who did survive the siege, was able to confirm many of the events that occurred during the fighting.)

The last day for the defenders of the Alamo was March 6, 1836.

The day dawned bright, clear, and cool. Inside the fortress little attempt was made to prepare breakfast. Supplies and ammunition were both perilously low, and the defenders knew a final crisis was at hand.

Outside the Alamo walls, the Mexicans seemed more than usually active. Lookouts on the fortress walls sensed a major attack was about to be launched, and they alerted their comrades.

Then, suddenly, a sharp, clear, and deadly trumpet call sounded in the Mexican encampment. It was the dreaded *degüello*—no quarter to the enemy! (The *degüello* was an old Moorish battle call, coming from a word meaning "to cut the throat.") Santa Anna himself had ordered the call to be sounded, having earlier remarked to one of his aides, "In this battle, there are to be no prisoners."

The Mexicans attacked in waves that seemed endless. They assaulted the Alamo from all sides. Twice they were beaten back, falling in great grainlike wind-rows before the musket and cannon fire of the defenders. The third attack was concentrated on the weakened north wall, and within moments the wall had been breached.

Swarming through the breach and into the main courtyard, the Mexicans stormed a central defense point called the Long Barracks. Colonel Travis, a single shot through his forehead, fell dead across one cannon. Other defenders were killed by grapeshot, musket fire, and bayonets—but not before taking a fearful toll of their attackers.

Davy Crockett was among the last of the defenders to fall, and he took a number of the enemy with him. Standing next to the chapel wall and guarding the entrance to it, Crockett soon ran out of ammunition. Then, using his rifle as a club, he fought off his attackers. Finally, his body riddled with bullets and slashed by sabers, Crockett fell. Around him in a semi-circle lay more than a dozen dead Mexicans.

Bowie had been placed on his cot just inside the chapel, along with Mrs. Dickinson, her baby, and the other civilians. As the Mexicans sprang into the chapel, Bowie emptied a rifle and then a pair of pistols at them. Out of ammunition, Bowie sat up on his cot and slashed about at his attackers with his famed knife. Finally Bowie, too, was dead, along with several of his attackers, who lay sprawled across his cot. Mrs. Dickinson, her baby, and the other noncombatants were spared.

David Crockett

Within a matter of hours the Alamo had fallen. But Santa Anna had paid a fearful price, almost 1,600 of his men having died. The Mexican general made every effort to minimize his losses, calling the battle "a small affair." And then, partly out of a spirit of revenge, he ordered the bodies of the fallen Alamo defenders to be stacked like cordwood outside the fortress walls. Oil was poured over the bodies and set afire. This was a funeral pyre that was to set all of Texas ablaze.

Santa Anna added fuel to this holocaust just three weeks later, when he and his forces moved on to Goliad. There he ruthlessly ordered the massacre of some 300 American prisoners who had been captured by the Mexicans in a fight at nearby Coleto Creek.

But the Texans, too, were to have their revenge. A month and a half after the Alamo fell, General Sam Houston, another renowned Texas patriot, led a small army of 800 men against Santa Anna and a force of 1,300 Mexicans at San Jacinto. As they rode into battle, the Texans shouted, "Remember the Alamo! Remember Goliad!" So fierce was the no-quarter attack of the Americans that the Mexicans surrendered in droves, throwing away their arms and begging for mercy, insisting, "Me no Alamo! Me no Goliad!" Within less than an hour, Sam Houston's men had routed the Mexican army, killing 630 while losing only 8. Among the Mexican prisoners was Santa Anna himself.

"The Fall of the Alamo" (painting by Theodore Gentilz—1844)

11

Sam Houston

The victory at San Jacinto marked Texas's true emergence as an independent and free republic on April 21, 1836. This, in turn, would lead to the annexation of Texas by the United States on December 29, 1845, and the annexation of Texas would be the immediate cause for an all-out war between the United States and Mexico, beginning in 1846.

2
Gunfire Along
the Rio Grande

The Alamo (*álamo* means "cottonwood" in Spanish) had originally been a Catholic mission surrounded by cottonwood trees. It was founded early in the eighteenth century by Father Antonio Olivares to bring religion and European civilization to the Indians. It was one of a series of missions and fortresses spread throughout the area by the Spanish during their early conquest of Mexico.

Mexico gained its independence from Spain in 1821. At that time the territory of Texas was a Mexican province, and San Antonio, home of the Alamo, was its capital. The Mexicans at first encouraged Americans to move into Texas, and Stephen F. Austin officially established an American colony there in 1822. Many other colonizers, called *empresarios,* soon followed, until the Mexicans began to be uneasy about the growing number of Americans in their midst. Im-

Mission San Antonio de Valero, built by the Spanish before Mexico gained its independence from Spain in 1821

15

migration to Texas from the United States was stopped by Mexico in 1830, and for the next several years relations between the American settlers and the Mexicans grew more and more strained.

In 1834 General Santa Anna seized political and military control of Mexico and became the nation's president-dictator. Santa Anna was one of Mexico's most colorful as well as most controversial figures. Regarded as a military hero and great statesman by many of his countrymen, he was despised by many others. Most Americans hated him, but his favor was sought by many American politicians, including at least one U.S. president, James Knox Polk.

Santa Anna was born at Jalapa, Mexico, in 1795. While still in his teens, he joined the Spanish army stationed in Mexico. During the early part of Mexico's struggle for independence from Spain, Santa Anna fought against the Mexicans. Later, in a move that was somehow typical of his personality, he changed sides and fought against the Spanish, becoming commander in chief of the Mexican army. It was while he was serving in this role that he first took over control of Mexico. He was to become his country's president-dictator several times, each time being overthrown and exiled, only to return once again. In the end he would die in poverty in Mexico City, blind and minus a leg lost in battle.

Mexico had hoped that it would be able to absorb all of the American colonists who had migrated there, but the year after Santa Anna first came to power, the Texas colonists declared their independence. Alarmed when San Antonio fell to the Texans in December, 1835, Santa Anna led his army there to put down the revolt. The immediate results were the Alamo massacre, the slaughter of American prisoners at Goliad, and then—in a complete reversal of fortune—Santa Anna's defeat and capture by Sam Houston at the Battle of San Jacinto.

After Santa Anna was taken prisoner at San Jacinto, several of his captors wanted to hang him, but Houston saved his life. In return, Houston had him sign an agreement recognizing the independence of Texas. Santa Anna was then allowed to return to Mexico City, where he promptly denied the agreement, saying he had signed it only because he had been forced to do so at gunpoint. The Mexican government also declared the agreement null and void, but Santa Anna was forced from office for the concessions he had made to the Americans.

During its decade as an independent republic, Texas grew and prospered. Sam Houston was named its first president, and he spoke for most Texans when he urged that the United States annex Texas. But the question of the annexation was a thorny one, filled with both national and international complications.

First of all, any talk of annexation angered the Mexican government since it did not recognize the in-

The Alamo Today

dependence of Texas and refused to think of it as anything but an integral part of Mexico. Secondly, there was the matter of slavery. All of the Southern states wanted to admit Texas to the Union because it permitted slavery. The Northern states were opposed to the admission of Texas for the same reason. Finally, great international pressure was brought against the annexation of Texas by both France and Great Britain, who feared the growing power of the United States in the western hemisphere. Eventually, the dispute with Britain over certain territorial and boundary rights and claims, especially those in Oregon, were to come close to starting another war with that country, as well as with Mexico. But the major problem continued to be the controversy with Mexico about who was to control Texas.

James Knox Polk entered the White House as the United States' eleventh president on March 4, 1845. He firmly supported the annexation of Texas, believing that it was the nation's "manifest destiny" to expand throughout North America and beyond.*

Polk also wanted California and New Mexico for the United States and offered to buy them from Mexico, to whom they belonged. But Mexico, furious over

* The term "Manifest Destiny" had been used for the first time by New York newspaper editor John L. O'Sullivan in the same year that Polk took office. For its important role in future American wars, see two other books in this series, *The United States in the Indian Wars* and *The United States in the Spanish-American War*.

Stephen Austin, who established an early American colony in Texas
PHOTO: SAN JACINTO MUSEUM OF HISTORY

the threatened annexation of Texas, not only refused to sell California and New Mexico but also broke off diplomatic relations with the United States when Polk took office.

The United States officially annexed Texas and it became the twenty-eighth state on December 29, 1845. There immediately arose another strong dispute regarding the actual boundary between Texas and Mexico. The United States claimed that the southern and southwestern boundary of Texas extended to the Rio Grande River, while Mexico claimed the southern border of Texas was at the Nueces River. As war threats grew, Polk ordered General Zachary Taylor to move his 4,000 U.S. Army troops to a position in southern Texas along the Rio Grande. The Mexicans regarded this move as an invasion of their territory by a foreign power and threatened to attack if the United States did not remove its troops below the Nueces.

Through the U.S. minister to Mexico, John Slidell, Polk countered with an offer to buy the no-man's-land between the Nueces and Rio Grande rivers, as well as California and New Mexico, but war fever was now running high in Mexico and Polk's offer was regarded as an insult. To accept it would be an act of treason. The Mexican government refused to meet with Slidell.

Late in April, 1846, there was a border clash along the Rio Grande between General Taylor's forces and Mexican forces under General Mariano Arista. Several American soldiers were killed, and General Taylor sent a message to Washington saying that "hostilities may now be considered as commenced."

On his part, General Arista declared, "I have had the pleasure of being the first to start the war."

General Taylor's message took two weeks to reach Washington. Polk immediately prepared a war message to Congress, stating flatly that the Mexicans had "shed American blood upon American soil. War exists by Mexico's act."

By May 11, Congress had approved a war bill. Polk signed it into law on May 13, 1846. War with Mexico was a reality.

Meanwhile, even before war had actually been declared, full-scale fighting had broken out on the Mexican border north of the Rio Grande, and Taylor's forces had won two small but important engagements—the Battle of Palo Alto and the Battle of Resaca de la Palma.

When Taylor had first been ordered to the Rio Grande by President Polk, he had moved his forces from Corpus Christi to Point Isabel on the coast, where they could be supplied and supported by U.S. naval vessels in the Gulf of Mexico. Establishing Point Isabel as his supply base, Taylor had then moved on to a point on the Rio Grande opposite the Mexican town of Matamoros. There he had built a fort. It was here that American and Mexican troops had first clashed in late April and Taylor had sent his war alert to Washington.

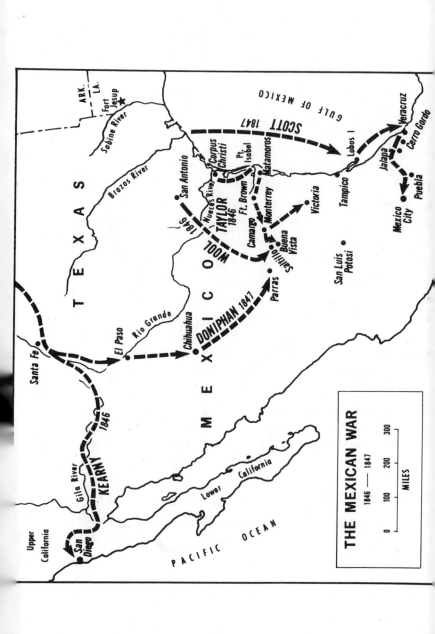

ARK. LA.

Fort Jesup ★

Sabine River

GULF OF MEXICO

T E X A S

Brazos River

San Antonio

Nueces River

Corpus Christi

Pt. Isabel

Ft. Brown

Matamoros

TAYLOR 1846

SCOTT 1847

Lobos I.

Veracruz

Cerro Gordo

Jalapa

Tampico

Puebla

Mexico City

San Luis Potosi

Buena Vista

Saltillo

Victoria

Monterrey

Camargo

Parras

1846

100M

Santa Fe

El Paso

Rio Grande

Chihuahua

DONIPHAN 1847

M E X I C O

KEARNY

1846

Gila River

Upper California

San Diego

Lower California

California

PACIFIC OCEAN

THE MEXICAN WAR

1846 — 1847

0   100   200   300

MILES

While that message was being carried to President Polk, the Mexicans continued to build up their forces at Matamoros. Early in May, Taylor moved most of his command back to Point Isabel, leaving a small detachment at the fort, under the command of Major Jacob Brown, for whom the fort was later named. Taylor made this move because he feared the Mexicans might surround the fort and cut off communications with his main supply base at Point Isabel.

A few days later, following a heavy bombardment of the fort during which Major Brown was killed, thousands of Mexicans crossed the Rio Grande. But they did not attack the fort. Instead, they circled around it and headed for Point Isabel.

Taylor immediately moved out to meet the advancing Mexicans. American troops numbered about 2,300 men, including both infantry and artillery. Mexican infantry, cavalry, and artillery numbered some 6,000. Despite the fact that they were outnumbered by more than two to one, Taylor's forces moved unhesitatingly against the Mexican line of battle, which had one flank stationed on a ridge called Palo Alto.

Almost immediately, the battle turned into an artillery duel, with the American gunners proving far more accurate and deadly in their fire than their Mexican counterparts. Several Mexican columns of infantry were cut to pieces by the rapid fire from the American artillery. When the Mexicans tried a cavalry attack, they lost their way in the dense black smoke

Hand-to-hand combat in an early battle of the Mexican War

PHOTO: U.S. ARMY

caused by a fierce grass fire that had been started by gunfire. Under cover of the smoke, the American artillery took up new positions and began to rain down death and destruction on the faltering Mexican forces. By nightfall, the Mexicans had fallen back beyond Palo Alto, having suffered more than 700 casualties, 320 of whom had been killed. American losses were 9 men killed and 47 wounded.

Taylor waited until dawn before resuming the attack. Then he ordered his troops forward. They moved down the road just a few miles to a point where the Mexicans had established a defensive position, in a dry creek bed called the Resaca de la Palma.

This was an extremely strong position, since the bank of the creek bed served as a natural defensive breastwork, and the Mexican artillery was zeroed in on the main road. Without hesitation, however, Taylor ordered his fast-moving artillery—now called "flying artillery"—to advance and engage the Mexican artillery. As this duel began, Taylor ordered his infantry to move forward, through the brush along the road, and then sent his cavalry dragoons at a full gallop straight down the road into the teeth of the Mexican fusillade of defensive fire.

This fierce frontal assault was too much for the Mexicans. The artillery men were driven from their guns, but, as the American cavalry rode on by, the Mexicans bravely returned. Seeing this, General Taylor galloped his horse to the front of his infantry columns and roared:

Battle of Resaca de la Palma. General Taylor gives one of his officers the order to charge the Mexican batteries.

"Damn it, take those guns and hold onto them!"

Grimly, the infantry, bayonets at the ready, moved forward, retook the guns, and held onto them. Within the hour the entire Mexican line broke and fled, racing toward the Rio Grande. As they passed Fort Brown, they again had to undergo cross fire from the fort's defenders, causing more casualties. In complete disorder, the fleeing Mexicans finally made it to the river, which they were able to cross before Taylor's forces could regroup and capture them.

American losses in the second day's battle were 33 killed and 89 wounded. Mexican losses were more than 1,000 killed, wounded, and drowned attempting to cross the Rio Grande.

It took Taylor until the middle of May to gather enough boats to move his troops across the Rio Grande. When he finally did so, he found the Mexicans had fled from Matamoros and disappeared into the interior. Taylor proceeded to occupy the town.

Meanwhile, shortly after war was declared, word had reached Washington of the American victories at Palo Alto and Resaca de la Palma. It caused a stir throughout the nation. War had scarcely begun and already the United States had Mexico on the run! Taylor was hailed as a hero throughout the land, and his name began to be talked of for the presidency. He was decorated and promoted from brigadier to major general, and most of his command were similarly honored.

But neither Taylor nor his superior, Commanding General of the Army Winfield Scott, who was stationed in Washington, were foolish enough to think, as did President Polk, that this would be a "quick war." Both Taylor and Scott were old and experienced campaigners, and they both knew what a long and difficult war this would be. They also knew how poorly prepared the United States was to fight it.

3
America Goes to War

"Let our arms now be carried with a spirit which shall teach the world that America knows how to crush as well as to expand!" Those were the words that appeared in a New York newspaper, the Brooklyn *Daily Eagle,* the day after war with Mexico was declared. They were written by the famed poet Walt Whitman.

While Whitman's words accurately expressed America's spirit of Manifest Destiny, they failed to note that the United States had very little military power with which to crush anything or anybody. As had happened so often in the past, and would happen so often in the future, the United States entered the war with great enthusiasm and not much else. The country was, in fact, almost completely unprepared to fight a single major battle, let alone a major war.

On the day war with Mexico was officially declared, the United States had only 7,000 men under arms, despite the fact that the entire U.S. Army at this time was the largest it had been since the War of 1812. More than half of the army was on duty in Texas with General Taylor, leaving only 3,000 troops to defend the entire length of the Rio Grande and the Canadian border, and to man numerous fortresses in Indian-fighting territory. And despite the fact that war clouds had been gathering on the horizon for months, virtually nothing had been done to expand the nation's armed forces. As a matter of fact, Congress was seriously considering closing down the military academy at West Point!

Included in Polk's war bill, however, was an appropriation of $10,000,000 and authorization to recruit 50,000 men to fight the war. These volunteers were allowed to enlist for periods of up to one year, an indication that the War Department expected the war to be a short one. These short-term enlistments were to cause serious problems, just as they had as far back as George Washington's time during the American Revolution.*

Most of the first volunteer troops came from the Southern and Southwestern states. This was so they could be quickly trained and sent to join General Taylor's command, on the southern Rio Grande, at Fort Brown and Matamoros. Other volunteers were re-

* See, in this series, *The American Revolution: America's First War for Independence*.

cruited throughout the United States to be trained and made available when needed.

In a few short weeks Taylor and his staff officers were all but overwhelmed with thousands of poorly trained and completely undisciplined recruits. This created serious problems because few of the Regular Army officers had any experience in training large bodies of troops.

Nevertheless, a training program was soon started, and drilling and target practice took place daily from sunup to sundown. A few of the training companies were equipped with new percussion-cap muskets, but most were forced to use flintlocks, much like those used in the Revolution and the War of 1812.

One of the officers in charge of recruit training was a young lieutenant named Ulysses S. Grant, future commander of all the Union armies in the Civil War and eighteenth U.S. president. Grant was one of three future U.S. presidents who served in the Mexican War. The other two were Franklin Pierce and Zachary Taylor. In addition, there was the future president of the Confederate States of America, Jefferson Davis. Davis was a colonel in the Mexican War; he was also General Taylor's son-in-law.

Endless drilling and teaching recruits in the traditional School of the Soldier soon began to pay dividends, so much so that Grant was later to comment, "A better army, man for man, never faced an enemy."

Recreation was all but nonexistent for the men in training, and, with their $7-a-month pay, few could afford to buy "luxuries" from the merchants who set up business in wagons outside the camps. Liquor, however, was all too readily available, and this caused additional discipline problems.

In order to provide the troops with some simple form of entertainment, theaters and acting groups were organized. In one of the training-camp plays, *The Moor of Venice,* Lieutenant Grant was cast in a female role opposite Lieutenant Theodoric Porter, who played the Moor. Porter complained so loudly at how poorly Grant acted as the female lead that a professional actress from New Orleans was hired to replace Grant—much to Grant's relief.

Not only were there future U.S. presidents in this fledgling U.S. Army that was about to embark on war with Mexico, but there was also an honor roll of men who would earn their military spurs in fighting together against the Mexicans, only to go on to even greater glory—in many instances, fighting against each other—in that American holocaust that lay just a few years ahead, the Civil War. Among future Civil War Northerners, in addition to Grant, Pierce, and Taylor, were Winfield Scott, George H. Thomas, William T. Sherman, John E. Reynolds, Winfield S. Hancock, George B. McClellan, Irvin McDowell, Joseph Hooker, and George Mcade. Future leading Civil War

Southerners, in addition to Davis, included Albert Sidney Johnston, Thomas "Stonewall" Jackson, Pierre Beauregard, Joseph Johnston, James L. Longstreet, and the future commander in chief of the Confederate armies, Robert E. Lee.

Living conditions in the training camps were primitive. During the dry, hot weather, drill, target practice, and breaking and riding horses kept the men occupied. (Herds of wild mustangs roamed the prairies near the Southern training camps, and the recruits either captured these or bought mounts from friendly Mexicans.)

But with the onset of cold, wet weather, most such activities ceased, and the men had little to do but stay inside their leaky tents and try to keep warm. Good drinking water was scarce; food was also scarce, and what there was was bad; and many of the recruits had little knowledge of how to maintain proper sanitary conditions in their camps. As a result, serious illness in the form of chest colds, fever, and dysentery soon struck down most of the volunteers. Weakened by these illnesses, many men died of what were normally minor diseases, such as measles. During the entire course of the war, about one in ten of the volunteers died from illness and disease.

General Taylor, however, regarded such harsh conditions as normal for a soldier. The son of a Revolutionary War officer, Taylor had spent most of his life at Army frontier posts during the War of 1812 and while fighting Indians in the old Northwest Territory and Florida. Abraham Lincoln had served under him during the Black Hawk War, where Taylor had earned the nickname "Old Rough and Ready."

In Mexico, as they had elsewhere, Taylor's men loved him. He shared all discomforts with them, eating the same food, living in a tent as leaky as any of theirs, and most of the time wearing a uniform as muddy and shabby as the rawest recruit's. His men also loved Taylor's horse, Old Whitey, which the general—one leg hooked over the saddle horn—would ride lazily through camp, stopping to talk with a drill squad, borrowing or offering a chew of tobacco, and encouraging his men about the battles that lay ahead. One of the things Taylor had to guard against on these visits was the men stealing hairs out of Old Whitey's tail. They thought a hair from Old Whitey's tail would bring good luck. A few years later, when Taylor became president, he brought Old Whitey with him to the White House and pastured him on the White House lawn. Washington youngsters often came by to ask if they could ride him, and they also tried to steal hairs from Old Whitey's tail.

While General Taylor was easygoing and did not seem to be a hard taskmaster, he did demand top performance from his men in battle. To this end, he trained them to take great pride in their roles as combat soldiers. By the late summer of 1846, Taylor told his troops, they would be setting out to capture Monterrey, Mexico. It would not be an easy campaign. The men set to work with a will to prepare for it.

Before the march on Monterrey could begin, however, there were diplomatic moves being made in Washington aimed at bringing the war to an end scarcely before it had begun.

4
The March on Monterrey

Since Santa Anna had fallen from power, he had been living in exile in Cuba, and Mariano Paredes was president of Mexico. President Polk thought that peace could be restored if Santa Anna were returned to power. One of Santa Anna's aides had, in fact, told Polk this—or so Polk later said.

As a result, Polk had Secretary of the Navy George Bancroft give orders to American ships in the Gulf of Mexico that Santa Anna was to be allowed to return to Mexico if he tried to do so. Word of this "safe conduct" was then passed to Santa Anna, in Havana, as well as to those forces in Mexico who remained loyal to him.

In early August, 1846, the Paredes government was overthrown by Santa Anna loyalists. By mid-August, Santa Anna had left Cuba; he landed safely at Veracruz and shortly thereafter resumed command of the

Mexican army. He promptly forgot whatever promises he had made to Polk—or Polk thought he had made—and began to prepare to meet General Taylor's invasion from the north.

It was diplomatic blunders such as this—and they continued throughout the conflict—that began to turn the American public's enthusiasm to anger and disgust. "Mr. Polk's War" was gradually to become the most unpopular war in American history up to the Vietnam conflict.

Nevertheless, while he was in the midst of negotiating with Santa Anna, Polk did tell his aides to sit down and work out war plans with Commanding General Winfield Scott.

During the course of a long and honorable Army career, Scott was to have the unique distinction of being the only American to serve as a general officer in three wars—the War of 1812, the Mexican War, and the Civil War. Called "Old Fuss and Feathers," his only military fault seemed to be that he was overly insistent on "preparedness" before committing troops to battle. It was this attitude that was to cause friction between him and President Polk from the opening gun of the Mexican War.

In early conferences with Polk and his aides, General Scott realized that Polk had no clear idea of war aims beyond seizing all Mexican land north of the Rio Grande and Gila rivers and westward to the Pacific Ocean. The overall war plan that was developed under

General Winfield Scott—Old Fuss and Feathers

Scott's direction included an overland operation, plus a naval blockade of key points on the Mexican coast. The overland operation was to consist of a three-pronged offensive. Taylor would advance on Monterrey, Mexico, while another force would attack Chihuahua from San Antonio. The third attack, under Colonel Stephen Kearny, was to head west from Fort Leavenworth and take Santa Fe, New Mexico, and then the whole of California. The capture of California was to be aided by the U.S. Navy in the Pacific. At this time, no plans were made for the offensive that Scott himself was to lead against Mexico City—an offensive that would eventually end the war.

By the late summer of 1846, Scott was glad to be able to tell Polk that General Taylor was ready to begin the first thrust of the land operation—the march on Monterrey.

Taylor knew that the country between Matamoros and Monterrey was a dry and waterless wasteland. Instead of marching his men all the way across this desert, Taylor decided to move them at least part of the way by boat. He could do this by transporting them, in shallow-draft steamboats, 130 miles up the Rio Grande to the town of Camargo. The U.S. quartermaster general, Thomas S. Jesup, performed a superhuman feat in furnishing Taylor with twenty of the necessary steamboats, and this small fleet successfully moved the attack force to Camargo. The force numbered about 6,000 men, two-thirds regulars and one-third volunteers. From Camargo there was a 150-mile march to their final destination. By September 19, this grim trek had been completed, and Taylor and his army stood before the city of Monterrey.

General Santa Anna, who remained in Mexico City, had given General Pedro de Ampudia the responsibility of defending this key city. Ampudia had more than 7,000 well-trained defenders at his command, and they had prepared the defenses well. They were aided by the fact that Monterrey was a natural fortress situated in a mountainous area. Its rear was protected by the Santa Catarina River, plus a series of foothills. Its other approaches were guarded by several very high hills, which the Mexicans had strongly fortified. More than forty pieces of heavy artillery looked down from these heights on any attacking forces that might move against the city along several of the main roads.

Once inside the city, the Americans would have no easy time of it, either. Monterrey's civilian population numbered about 15,000 persons, most of whom lived in stone-walled houses, each one of which was something of a small fortress in itself. As Taylor and his scouts surveyed the scene, Taylor commented:

"Looks like we'll have to dig 'em out with bayonets."

General Taylor's plan of attack was to divide his forces, sending 2,000 regulars, under General William Worth, on a flanking movement around the city, while Taylor himself attacked the city from the front with the main body of troops. The purpose of Worth's flanking movement was to seize control of a road that led from the town of Saltillo to Monterrey and along which all Mexican supplies and reinforcements would have to travel.

There were preliminary skirmishes on Sunday, September 20, but the fierce four-day battle did not begin in earnest until the next morning. On Sunday night it rained heavily, and under cover of the darkess and rain, Worth was able to move his men close to the Saltillo road before they were discovered by the enemy. The Mexicans tried to break through Worth's lines with a cavalry charge backed up by an infantry attack, but the fast-moving, rapid-firing, and highly accurate American artillery, plus deadly rifle fire from the American infantry, shattered the Mexican charge. Shortly after daybreak, the Saltillo road was in American hands. Worth had lost fewer than twenty men.

Meanwhile, General Taylor was launching a series of diversionary attacks to prevent Ampudia from shifting his main forces to concentrate on Worth's flanking movement. Taylor sent part of his men forward to capture the fortified positions on top of the several high hills. The most important of these included two truly formidable bastions, one called the Black Fort and the other Fort Tenería (or, as the Americans called it, the Tannery).

Taylor sent separate forces of regulars on frontal assaults against these all-but-impregnable positions.

Old Rough and Ready (from a painting)

Led by such officers as Colonel Jefferson Davis and Lieutenant Ulysses Grant, the men charged bravely into the deadly enemy fire from behind the loopholed fortress walls. Both attacks ground to a halt when American artillery fire failed to damage the fortress walls.

A second attack was launched, then a third—but these, too, failed, and the field was strewn with American dead and wounded.

Taylor now assigned volunteer regiments to join the regulars in a last, desperate assault. They also advanced without hesitation, this time covered by heavy and accurate American artillery fire.

The first fortress to fall was the Tannery. Its defenders began to give way when a wall was battered down and American sharpshooters began to pick off the Mexican officers. As the defenders began to falter, Jefferson Davis shouted to his Southern volunteers:

"Now, men, now! Give me thirty men with knives, and I'll take the fort!"

Not thirty men with knives but two regiments of volunteers from Tennessee and Mississippi, brandishing bayonets, charged the fortress in a final rush that swept the enemy before them. By nightfall, American control of the Tannery was consolidated, but it had cost 400 American casualties.

The next day, Ampudia kept control of the Black Fort, but he moved the rest of his troops into the stone houses surrounding Monterrey's main plaza.

Now Taylor's troops had the unenviable and murderous task of house-to-house fighting. Most of the men realized it meant sudden death to attempt an attack by charging up the main streets. If they did so, the Mexican defenders would simply remain inside the houses and pick off every American in sight. The only possible way to drive the Mexicans to retreat into the plaza was to blast through the wall of each house with artillery fire, and then move in with axes, shovels, and crowbars, and hammer down whatever stone protection remained. In this way, knocking down walls or burrowing through them, the Americans fought on for another day, driving the Mexicans yard by yard before them.

Finally, on September 24, General Ampudia sent word that he would surrender. It took one more day to decide on terms, and then the American flag was hoisted over Monterrey—one of America's first victories on foreign soil along the route of Manifest Destiny.

General Taylor had won yet another resounding victory, but he and his men would have little chance to enjoy it. The surrender terms would be instantly rejected by President Polk in Washington, and Taylor was to be severely criticized by the administration for agreeing to them. Nevertheless, the victorious march on Monterrey was to be Taylor's first major step on the road to the White House.

5
The March of Doniphan's Thousand

When General Ampudia had first asked for terms to yield Monterrey, General Taylor had said the terms were unconditional surrender. Ampudia then asked to meet with Taylor for further discussion. This discussion led to a complete surrender of the city by Ampudia, plus the withdrawal of all Mexican troops. However, Ampudia also got Taylor to agree to an eight-week armistice.

It was the length of this armistice that angered Polk and the rest of his administration. They felt that Taylor should have followed up his victory immediately with a deeper thrust into Mexico.

"In agreeing to this armistice," Polk wrote in his diary, "General Taylor violated his express orders, and I regret that I cannot approve of his course. He had the enemy in his power and should have taken them prisoners. It will enable the Mexican army to reorganize and recruit so as to make another stand."

Actually, Polk's irritation was mainly due to the fact that it was now publicly known that he had tried to work out a scheme with Santa Anna that would result in the peaceful surrender of Mexico, but Santa Anna had tricked him and now seemed determined to wage a major war. This meant that more men, money, and material would have to be poured into the American war effort, and Polk was not certain the American people and the Congress would support him. He also feared both General Taylor and General Scott as possible political opponents for the presidency in the next national election. General Taylor's name was already on everybody's lips, and General Scott's popularity would probably be equally great if he led another major expeditionary force to Mexico, which was what Scott had been planning to do. This was to be an amphibious operation, with Veracruz as the landing point. Polk determined not to let Scott take charge of this expedition.

On his part, General Scott defended Taylor to Polk, pointing out that Taylor's small army had suffered 500 casualties and was down to no more than 5,000 effective soldiers, since many of his men were also ill. In addition, Taylor's ammunition and other supplies were low, and his supply lines were dangerously stretched, since he was in command of an isolated army deep in enemy country.

Nevertheless, Polk immediately canceled the armistice. This, in turn, infuriated Taylor, but, like the good soldier he was, he prepared to go back into action.

General Zachary Taylor
PHOTO: U.S. ARMY

He first notified General Ampudia that the armistice had ended, and then sent General Worth against the town of Saltillo, which Worth took in mid-November, 1846, against light opposition. Taylor then made his army headquarters nearby and awaited further orders from Washington. His main problem was what place to attack next.

While Taylor waited, the other thrusts in the overall land operation were all proceeding according to plan.

By the late summer of 1846, General John E. Wool, with a force of some 2,000 men, had left San Antonio. Their original goal had been Chihuahua, but following Taylor's success at Monterrey, Wool's command was directed to join up with Taylor's forces at Saltillo.

At Fort Leavenworth, Colonel Stephen Kearny had assembled his Army of the West and by mid-June was ready for the long march to New Mexico and California. Kearny's army numbered about 2,500 men, including 850 mounted volunteers from Missouri commanded by a tall, lanky, red-haired peacetime lawyer, Colonel Alexander Doniphan.

The Army of the West set off on the first leg of its march, a 537-mile trek from Fort Leavenworth to Bent's Fort, on June 22. It arrived there on July 29, having struggled through some of the hottest, driest, dustiest country in America. The Mexicans had an apt name for such a march—the "Journey of the

Dead," they called it, or simply *jornada*. U.S. soldiers were to experience many *jornadas* in their Mexican campaigns but none quite so severe as the one Colonel Doniphan and his Missouri volunteers were soon to set out on.

From Bent's Fort, Kearny's command continued toward Santa Fe, New Mexico's capital, where they expected to encounter stout resistance from Mexican forces under New Mexico's governor, Manuel Armijo. Leaving Bent's Fort on August 2, the Army of the West marched for more than two straight weeks from dawn to dusk, covering another 320 miles and arriving at Apache Canyon near Santa Fe on August 18. They had traveled more than 850 miles from Fort Leavenworth in less than two months—but harsher trials were yet to come.

Kearny and his men had expected Apache Canyon to be heavily fortified, since it was an ideal defense position. The road through the canyon, down which any advancing army would have to travel, was carved between steep walls and could easily be commanded by artillery placed on the nearby heights. Governor Armijo had indeed succeeded in enlisting several thousand Mexicans and Indians to defend Santa Fe at the canyon, but when Kearny's army appeared on the scene, the defenders fled. Kearny and his men then marched into Santa Fe, where the American flag was raised over the governor's adobe palace, and Kearny took over as military governor. His first act was to announce the annexation of New Mexico by the United States. The American soldiers were greeted with apparent warmth by the local Mexicans and Indians—a mood that was not to last very long.

Kearny remained in Santa Fe until September 25. He then set out for California with several hundred mounted soldiers, leaving behind Colonel Doniphan and the Missouri volunteers as an occupying force to maintain American control over Santa Fe and the surrounding area.

When Kearny set out for California, he told Doniphan to wait in Santa Fe for the arrival of additional volunteers from Missouri under the command of Colonel Sterling Price. When Price and his men arrived, Doniphan and his troops were to head south toward El Paso and then on to Chihuahua to join up with General Wool. (Neither Kearny nor Doniphan knew that Wool's orders had since been changed, sending him to Saltillo.)

Doniphan spent a part of his time before Price arrived trying to pacify the Navajo and Ute Indians in the area around Santa Fe. Although they had seemed peaceful enough when the Americans first arrived, the Indians were now conducting raids on many New Mexican settlements, as well as on Santa Fe itself. The Indians regarded both the Mexicans and Americans as intruders in their territory and fought against both with equal fervor. Since New Mexico had now been annexed to the United States, it was the U.S. Army's duty to protect all settlers in the area. As an indication of how rapidly the New Mexicans accepted the fact that they were now U.S. citizens, Doniphan reported to Washington that Polk was referred to as *el presidente de nuestra república* ("the president of our republic").

Almost daily, Doniphan sent out columns of mounted Missourians into the nearby hills to try to meet and talk peace with the Indians. Finally, on November 22, Doniphan was successful in signing a major peace treaty with the Indians. By this time, Colonel Price had arrived, and Colonel Doniphan was ready to head south to El Paso.

Doniphan assembled his regiment at Valverde, along the Rio Grande, in early December, 1846. From there, he sent back word to Price at Santa Fe requesting a battalion of light artillery. Before the artillery arrived, Doniphan and his so-called Thousand—actually no more than 850 at this time—moved out on a wintry day in mid-December. Although it was dry in this region, it was also very cold because of the high altitude.

Just a few miles south of Valverde, the road to El Paso left the banks of the Rio Grande and moved 90 barren and waterless miles across the first *jornada* of this particular journey. Not only was there no water on this route, but it was also bitterly cold on the lofty plateau along which the road ran. Three days later, on December 22—thirsty, hungry, half-frozen—Doniphan and his men stumbled into the small Mexican town of Doña Ana. Here there was food and water for both men and animals, and Doniphan let his men rest for a day.

The march was resumed on December 24, and that night, Christmas Eve, Doniphan's Thousand went into camp on a small river that led to the Rio Grande. On Christmas Day, the men scattered along the river seeking fresh forage for the animals and fuel with which to make fires. It was while they were thus engaged, scattered and totally unprepared for combat, that they were suddenly attacked by an enemy infantry and cavalry force numbering 500 men, under the command of Colonel Antonio Ponce.

Despite the complete surprise of the attack, Doniphan's men raced for their weapons and were able to form an irregular defensive line. Ponce, had he pressed home the attack, would undoubtedly have completely overrun the Americans. Instead, he sent forward a messenger under a flag of truce demanding that Doniphan either surrender or face a "no-quarter" death charge.

Doniphan's reply was clear and simple: "Charge and be damned," he said.

The Mexican charge was accompanied by wild rifle fire at too distant a range to be effective. The Americans, however, held their fire until the enemy was only 150 yards away, and the results were shattering. The charge was halted in its tracks, and then

Doniphan sent in a flanking attack that drove the Mexicans into retreat. Forty-three Mexicans were killed and an unknown number wounded in the half-hour battle. Only seven Americans were slightly wounded by the enemy's wild fire.

The next day Doniphan's Thousand resumed the march toward El Paso.

Doniphan expected a battle at El Paso, but there was none, the enemy having fled before the advancing Americans. Arriving there after a 25-mile march, Doniphan and his men moved into the center of the town and set up their camp in the main plaza. Doniphan still had not received any artillery from Santa Fe and sent back word to Colonel Price to speed it along. It was another month before the artillery arrived, during which time Doniphan's Thousand relaxed and enjoyed the peacetime pleasures of the friendly Mexican town. But they began to be impatient with the delay.

The artillery finally arrived, and on February 8 Doniphan ordered his men toward Chihuahua. Including the men who had brought the artillery, Doniphan now had 925 soldiers in his command. But he was faced with a major problem. While in bivouac in El Paso, he had received word that General Wool would not join him in the major attack on Chihuahua. This meant that ahead of Doniphan and his men lay 250 miles of waterless waste, and there was no promise of reinforcements from any quarter. At the end of the journey he and his men would probably face a battle against an enemy force that outnumbered them several to one. Without additional orders should he proceed or retreat? Perhaps influenced by the fact that to retreat would be as difficult as to advance, he headed his columns of infantry troops, cavalry, and horsedrawn wagons toward Chihuahua.

Six days out of El Paso, Doniphan's Thousand hit a 75-mile stretch of deep sand. Before heading into this desert, the men filled everything that would hold liquid with water, including the scabbards that usually held their swords. The men not only had to get through the sand themselves, but they also had to aid the animals in dragging the supply wagons through it, taking turns at forcing the wheels to turn in the hub-deep sand by grasping the spokes and forcing them forward. Three days later, they reached their first water hole.

During the course of the next weeks there were half a dozen additional *jornadas* through which Doniphan's Thousand trudged their desperate way. Some were as little as 45 miles in length, others were as long as 100 miles. Finally, on Sunday, February 28, three weeks after leaving El Paso, they approached the Sacramento River—15 miles from Chihuahua. Here they encountered the enemy and the enemy's major defensive fortifications.

The several thousand Mexican defenders under the command of General José Heredia, who had been sent north by Santa Anna, had been well aware of

Doniphan's approach. Mexican scouts had been reporting daily the extent of the Americans' advance, and the defenses outside the city had been in a state of preparation for weeks. Cannon were zeroed in on all key approach roads, including the main El Paso road down which the Americans were traveling. Housing the Mexican artillery were several stone fortresses, garrisoned by 2,000 crack troops. At least 1,000 Mexican infantry—the Americans claimed there were more —were a part of General Heredia's reserve.

The major Mexican defenses were set up along the Sacramento River. On the near side of the Sacramento, facing the approaching Americans, there was a high plain, and in front of this plain there was a deep, dry river bed called the Arroyo Seco. The Mexican artillery was zeroed in on the plain. The Mexicans expected the Americans to be halted at the far edge of the dry river bed, whose banks were at least fifty feet high. Then, if the Americans struggled down the far bank, crossed the dry river bed, and scrambled up onto the plain, the Mexicans planned on bombarding them into submission.

That morning, realizing that they would soon be meeting the enemy, Doniphan had formed his command into four parallel columns of infantry, horse-drawn wagons, and cavalry. When they reached the dry arroyo, Doniphan did not halt. He ordered the four columns, wagons and all, over the edge of the bank. Infantrymen half ran and half slid to the bottom.

Cavalry horses stumbled and fell, but rose again to advance. Teams and wagons careened down the slopes and somehow managed to make it upright to the canyon floor. There, still in parallel columns, Doniphan's doughty Thousand raced across the dry river bed and made the heroic climb up the opposite bank. Here the infantry put its backs to the wheels of the wagons and manhandled them up the steep slope. In an amazingly short time, the four parallel columns had reassembled on the plain and were ready for the attack.

Had the Mexicans left their fortified positions along the Sacramento and advanced to attack the Americans as they struggled across the dry arroyo, the outcome of the battle would have been a disastrous defeat for the Americans. By deciding to let the Americans cross the canyon and assemble safely on the plain, the Mexicans gave up their greatest combat advantage by losing the initiative to Doniphan's Thousand.

Once the Americans had assembled on the plain, the Mexicans decided to leave their defensive positions and attack. But by then the Americans had not only a solid line of attack formed, but they also had their artillery in position and ready to fire.

An hour-long artillery duel started the battle. Then Doniphan ordered his cavalry to charge the Mexican positions. They were followed up by infantry, who moved to within a quarter of a mile of the enemy. The cavalry charge was unsuccessful on the flanks, but did manage a small break at the center of the Mexican line. American artillery, firing at close range, took advantage of this slight break, and then the entire American infantry line rolled forward like a wave, sweeping the enemy before it. The Mexicans held only briefly, then broke and ran. Many of the enemy tried to escape the deadly American fire by swimming down the Sacramento River. Most of these men were drowned.

Three hours after it began, the Battle of Sacramento had ended in an incredible American victory. Doniphan's Thousand had defeated a far superior force holding securely entrenched positions by sheer determination, bravery, and amazingly accurate firepower. Equally unbelievable were the casualty figures: The Americans had lost 1 man killed, and suffered 11 wounded. More than 300 Mexicans had died, and an equal number were wounded.

The day after the battle, the Mexican army abandoned Chihuahua, which was immediately occupied by Doniphan's command. But Doniphan was still at a loss as to what his further course of action should be. Still without new orders and uncertain as to where General Wool or General Taylor might be, Doniphan finally heard rumors of a major battle at Buena Vista, some 600 miles away. Assuming that it was Wool or Taylor engaged at Buena Vista, Doniphan sent a messenger there. Meanwhile, his troops acted as an army of occupation in Chihuahua, establishing an American military government in the heart of Mexico.

Two months later, word finally reached Doniphan, from General Taylor, ordering him and his men to join the main American army at Saltillo. Once again Doniphan and his men set out on what was to be the final leg of their long march. Doniphan and his Missouri volunteers had all originally enlisted for the term of one year. By the time they reached General Taylor at the main army camp, that year was almost up. When they left Taylor's camp, after passing in review before thousands of cheering fellow soldiers, they moved to the Rio Grande. There they took steamboats to the Gulf of Mexico and then sailed to New Orleans. At New Orleans they were given their discharges, but, perhaps best of all, they were given their pay—the first pay they had received in twelve long months. From New Orleans each man was allowed to make his own way back to Missouri. From the time they left home until the time they returned, each of Doniphan's Thousand had traveled more than 5,000 heroic miles. There have been few such feats in the history of the U.S. Army.

6
The Conquest
of California

When Stephen Kearny and his small detachment left Santa Fe for California in late September, 1846, they faced almost as grim a march as did Doniphan's Thousand on their way to Chihuahua. Kearny, just recently promoted to brigadier general, had orders to cooperate with any military units sent ashore by U.S. naval forces operating in the Pacific off the California coast. Together they were supposed to take control of California. How he was to do so, with such a small military force at his command, was not quite clear to Kearny, but he knew that California was sparsely populated and Mexico had no naval forces with which to fight the U.S. war fleet.

Nevertheless, Kearny was greatly relieved when, on their way to the west coast, he and his men met the famous scout and frontiersman Kit Carson, who was traveling to Washington to report that Commodore

Kit Carson
PHOTO: DENVER PUBLIC LIBRARY WESTERN HISTORY DEPARTMENT

Robert F. Stockton of the U.S. Navy, and military shore parties from Stockton's Pacific fleet, had seized California. When Kearny heard this welcome news, he sent most of his men back to Santa Fe, along with Carson's dispatches to be forwarded to Washington. Then Kearny got Kit Carson to guide him and 100 of his men to San Diego.

Kearny's march to California took more than two months. Fortunately, Carson advised Kearny to return his wagons to Santa Fe and travel only on foot and horseback, because their route took them along narrow trails unsuitable for wagons, through rugged mountain country in southern Arizona and across the continental divide. The final leg of their journey brought them down out of the mountains into desert country, and here they were faced with furnace-like heat and no water. Having lost most of their horses and pack mules, Kearny's force struggled into San Pasqual, thirty miles from San Diego, early in December. Here they learned that, while Commodore Stockton had indeed seized California, the Californians were now in a state of revolt against the United States.

The situation in California and the rest of the Pacific west coast area had been a politically complicated one for many years before the Mexican War. In addition to the United States, Great Britain, Spain (later Mexico), and Russia had laid claims to various parts of the region. Outstanding among these were Great Britain's claims to the Oregon Territory, which extended from Russian-owned Alaska to the northern California border.

Britain's rights to the Oregon Territory were largely based on the fur trade established there through the Hudson's Bay Company, but these claims were hotly disputed by the United States. For a time, Britain and the United States jointly shared the area, but the United States finally insisted on sole ownership for all land between the parallels of 42° north latitude and 54°40′. Polk had been elected on a political platform that included this agreement as one of its planks. After Polk was elected and Great Britain gave some indication of not living up to its part of the agreement, "Fifty-four forty, or fight!" became a national war cry. Fortunately, Great Britain finally agreed to the demarcation line between the United States and British territory, or the United States would have found itself fighting a war against Great Britain as well as Mexico.

Because of its problems with the British in the Oregon Territory, the United States suspected that Great Britain might also have designs on California. This was not true, but it provoked several serious incidents.

In 1842 Commodore Thomas C. Jones of the U.S. Navy thought that a British force was about to seize California. To prevent such a move, Jones landed at Monterey, California, and raised the American flag over the Mexican governor's palace. When Jones realized he had been misinformed, he hastily ordered the flag lowered, and he and the U.S. government extended apologies to the Mexican government. This incident very nearly provoked an outbreak of war.

The United States also used other means to take over the state. Polk had not been the only president to offer to buy California. President Andrew Jackson, in 1835, had also made an offer, which was bluntly refused by Mexico.

In 1845 Thomas Larkin, U.S. consul at Monterey, made strong but futile efforts to get California to secede from Mexico. At the same time the U.S. Navy in the Pacific was told to occupy California ports in case of a war with Mexico.

The final, and most mysterious, move in the continuing efforts of the United States to take over California by fair means or foul was the sending of a young Army officer, Captain John C. Frémont, on a so-called surveying expedition into the area—a surveying expedition that had all the earmarks of a military effort.

Frémont was already a famous explorer and pathfinder of the Pacific northwest before he set out on his California journey in the fall of 1845. His accurate early surveys had enabled settlers to travel over the Oregon Trail. The son-in-law of an important U.S. senator, Thomas Hart Benton, Frémont was extremely popular in Washington social and political circles. His activities in California led some people to believe that Frémont had visions of conquering California and handing it over to the United States, whereupon he would be elected to high political office—perhaps even the presidency.

Although he started out with only a handful of men, Frémont recruited men along the way, as well as in California when he arrived there. One of the first places he pitched camp on the west coast was near Monterey. Suspicious of Frémont's motives, local officials told him to leave the area. Frémont then moved north toward the border of Oregon. Here he received word from Washington that war with Mexico was threatening. He then returned south, and he and his men fought several minor skirmishes with the Mexicans in California.

Early in July, 1846, Frémont was responsible for the so-called Bear Flag Revolt. Encouraged by Frémont's promises of massive backing by the United States, a handful of Californians at the town of Sonoma declared that California was now independent and would in the future be known as the Bear Flag Republic. What Frémont hoped to gain from this comedy of errors has never been fully explained, but it is believed he hoped that the United States would annex the Bear Flag Republic, as it had annexed Texas. In any event, the Bear Flag Republic existed for only a few days. Word was soon received that the Mexican War had begun, and the Bear Flag was promptly lowered and the Stars and Stripes raised in its place. Frémont's Bear Flaggers later became the California battalion of the U.S. Army, with Frémont as their commander. He was promoted to major at this time.

When war was declared, U.S. Navy Commodore John D. Sloat moved into Monterey, California, and raised the American flag there. Shortly afterward, Sloat fell ill and was relieved by Commodore Stockton, who immediately took over the entire San Francisco area. A few weeks later, the Los Angeles area was occupied by Stockton's naval forces used as landing parties, and Frémont was put in charge of taking San Diego. San Diego also fell into American hands with scarcely a shot being fired, and Stockton moved his headquarters there. He then sent Kit Carson toward Washington with dispatches announcing the conquest of California.

It was at this point, however, that the entire situation began to unravel, and Stockton sent further word to Kearny at San Pasqual that California was in revolt.

Despite the weakened condition of his few troops when they arrived at San Pasqual, Kearny did not hesitate to advance. Kearny encountered the enemy at a road junction just outside San Pasqual, and a brief but bloody engagement followed. Kearny and his men drove the Mexicans from the road, but the cost was severe. Almost a third of his men were killed, and Kearny himself was wounded.

A few days later, what was left of Kearny's 100-man force struggled on toward San Diego. Along the way they encountered a small relief party sent to meet them by Commodore Stockton, and they finally made their way into San Diego on December 12.

Commodore Robert F. Stockton
PHOTO: CHICAGO HISTORICAL SOCIETY

Although Stockton had only a relatively small force at his command in San Diego, there were even fewer enemy troops in the area. Consequently, Stockton decided to leave a token force of defenders at San Diego while he and Kearny led a march on the beleaguered Los Angeles, where the Californians in revolt had retaken the city from the garrison Stockton had originally left there. Stockton had also wanted to use Frémont to help on this expedition, but Frémont had now left the area and was off somewhere—no one knew exactly where—"recruiting additional troops," as he put it.

Stockton's command numbered about 500 men, including soldiers, sailors, and marines. Kearny had now recovered sufficiently from his wounds so that he could accompany the expedition. In fact he wanted to command it, but Stockton retained that job as overall commander of the area, putting Kearny in charge of the infantry. This interservice rivalry and Stockton's favoritism toward Frémont later caused a complete break between Stockton and Kearny.

Leaving San Diego on December 29, Stockton met no enemy until he reached Los Angeles on January 8, 1847. There, on the banks of the San Gabriel River, he encountered strong enemy defenses, but he and his men ignored them and continued their march toward the city. When Stockton sent word to the city's defenders that he and his command intended to enter and destroy Los Angeles, the enemy launched two vigorous but unsuccessful attacks. When these attacks had been beaten off, Stockton continued to advance. On the morning of January 10, the enemy raised a flag of truce and offered to surrender.

At this point Major Frémont reappeared on the scene. He had indeed succeeded in enlisting several hundred additional men in his California battalion, from among American settlers in California, and now took charge of the surrender ceremonies as the "military commander" of the area. Actually, General Kearny far outranked Frémont, but Kearny was not at the immediate surrender scene, a ranch at Cahuenga. Technically, Commodore Stockton also outranked Major Frémont, but Stockton was a naval officer, and thus, Frémont pointed out, had no jurisdiction over a surrender on land. In any event, a peace treaty called the Treaty of Cahuenga was signed by Frémont and approved by Stockton on January 13, 1847.

Later Stockton even went so far as to appoint Frémont, instead of Kearny, governor. This so infuriated Kearny that, when Stockton left Los Angeles and took his fleet to sea, Kearny ordered Frémont back to Washington and had him court-martialed for insubordination. Frémont was found guilty, but President Polk reversed the court's decision, mainly because of the influence of Frémont's father-in-law, Senator Benton. Disgusted, Frémont resigned from the Army.

Although there were certain comic-opera aspects to the American conquest of California and its aftermath—most of them supplied by the colorful Major Frémont—it was a fact that the whole of California was now in the hands of the United States. What lay ahead was the complete conquest of Mexico via a landing at Veracruz and a march on Mexico City.

**7
American Atrocity
at Agua Nueva**

From the time of his first clash with the Mexicans along the Rio Grande, General Taylor had planned on being the commanding general who would lead the triumphant U.S. Army into a conquered Mexico City. But he had never been in favor of an 800-mile overland march against the Mexican capital. He had agreed with General Scott in Washington that an amphibious landing should be made on the east coast of Mexico, at Tampico or Veracruz, and the capital approached from there. Interestingly enough, even Mexican General Santa Anna had suggested this route to President Polk, when Santa Anna was pretending to work out a deal with Polk to hand over Mexico in return for his own "safe-conduct" passage from Cuba.

Polk finally agreed on the Veracruz expedition, but he did not want either of his two potential political opponents, General Taylor or General Scott, to lead it.

His first choice was his political ally, Senator Benton. Even Benton, however, saw the folly in naming a civilian, rather than an experienced military man, to head up such an important military campaign. Finally Polk was left with no choice but Taylor or Scott. He chose Scott, partially for political reasons—Scott was less of a political threat than Taylor—but also because Scott outranked Taylor, and Taylor was against landing at Veracruz during the height of the yellow fever (*el vómito*) season, which was now approaching.

After Scott was selected as commander of the Veracruz expedition, Polk expected him to go into action immediately. But Scott, true to his traditional method of highly detailed planning and preparation, lingered on in Washington. The truth of the matter was that the campaign actually demanded extremely careful and detailed planning. This would be the largest amphibious landing ever attempted by American military forces. Involved would be between 15,000 and 25,000 men, and transport alone was a major problem, let alone maintaining such a large force in enemy territory.

Nevertheless, Polk—liking Scott less each day—tried to drive the expedition's leader out of Washington. This, in turn, made Scott even more stubborn. He, too, was well aware of the political aspects of the situation. When Polk became too insistent, Scott told Secretary of War William Marcy, "I do not desire to place myself in that most perilous of all positions—a fire upon my rear from Washington, and a fire upon my front from the Mexicans."

Secretary Marcy finally convinced Scott that he should leave the problems of supplies, ammunition, and troop transports in the hands of the quartermaster general while Scott went to Mexico to meet with General Taylor. The purpose of this meeting was to decide what troops, and how many, Taylor could release to Scott to use against Veracruz and Mexico City. The war in the northern theater now appeared to be over, and there seemed no need to keep anything but a token holding force there.

But Taylor refused to meet with Scott. Angered at not being offered command of this major campaign of the war, and not wanting to be put in charge of a mere holding operation, Taylor avoided Scott by leading several minor military skirmishes into the countryside around Camargo, Monterrey, and Saltillo. This rash action could easily have been regarded as insubordination by a less generous commanding officer than Scott, who simply ignored Taylor's stubborn rudeness.

Scott, however, did have to inform Taylor that he was taking most of Taylor's regulars and half his volunteers—a total of some 8,000 men—away from him for the Veracruz–Mexico City campaign. This left Taylor with about 5,000 troops, all volunteers, plus small forces of cavalry and artillery with which to remain on the defensive. Scott told Taylor the news in two separate letters. Unfortunately, one of these letters fell into the hands of General Santa Anna when a courier, Lieutenant John A. Richey, was captured by the Mexicans. Realizing that Taylor's forces at Saltillo would be severely weakened by the withdrawal of so many of his troops, Santa Anna decided early in January, 1847, to launch a full-scale attack against Taylor at Saltillo.

At this time, Santa Anna was at a place called San Luis Potosí, where he had been assembling and training an army of some 20,000 men. Santa Anna had known about the Veracruz expedition for some time—mainly through newspaper reports—and, until he had read Scott's letter to Taylor, had intended to use his own army to defend Mexico City. Intelligence sources had reported Santa Anna's intentions to Taylor, so Taylor did not expect a major Mexican attack.

Nevertheless, Taylor was somewhat uneasy about such a large enemy force within striking distance of his own badly weakened army. Early in February, Taylor ordered all of his troops out of Saltillo to a camp twenty miles south of the city at a town called Agua Nueva. He made this move partly for defensive purposes and partly to boost the morale of his troops, who were bored to the point of mutiny with the long months of garrison duty they had been experiencing.

Maintaining discipline among volunteer troops was a major problem all during the Mexican War. This was especially true when the men had to serve as what amounted to occupation troops in towns and cities on foreign soil. Since they were outside the United States, civil laws could not apply to any crimes the soldiers might commit against the Mexican civilians. All infractions had to be dealt with by military courts, and these were all too often sympathetic and lenient with American soldiers who committed offenses against the Mexican civilian population. At Agua Nueva, a truly bloody atrocity was committed by volunteer troops, an atrocity that was something of a forerunner of similar atrocities that would be committed by U.S. soldiers in the Vietnam War at such places as the village of My Lai.

The incident at Agua Nueva grew out of a series of insults made to Mexican women by some Arkansas volunteers. In retaliation, on February 9, one of the Arkansas soldiers—or "Rackensackers," as they were nicknamed—was murdered. The Rackensackers responded to this deed by getting together a 100-man vigilante party to find and punish the murderers. At a nearby village, claiming they had found a piece of the dead man's equipment, the Rackensackers opened fire on the civilians, who tried to escape into a nearby cave. The Americans followed the Mexicans into the cave, still firing indiscriminately. Before the sound of firing brought other troops from Taylor's army to stop the massacre, more than 30 Mexican men, women, and children had been slain.

General Taylor's reaction was swift if somewhat tardy. Unable to obtain the identities of the specific

"Rackensackers on the Rampage," an artist's conception of the
American atrocity at Agua Nueva

soldiers involved, Taylor ordered the two companies to which the men belonged shipped home in disgrace. (Ironically, this order was never carried out because of the bravery of Arkansas troops at the Battle of Buena Vista, which followed.) His comment to the rest of his army was: "Such deeds cast indelible disgrace upon our arms and the reputation of our country." Lieutenant George Meade, a future Northern general in the Civil War, went a step farther in criticizing the volunteer troops and their elected officers. In a letter home, Meade wrote: "They are sufficiently well drilled for practical purposes, and are, I believe, brave, and will fight as gallantly as any men. But they are a set of Goths and Vandals, without discipline, laying waste to the country wherever they go; making us a terror to innocent people. If one of their number happens to get into a drunken brawl and is killed, they run over the country, killing all the poor, innocent people they find in their way, to avenge, as they say, the murder of their brother." Unfortunately, neither Taylor nor Meade nor any other American officers in the Mexican War seemed able to convince all of their troops that Mexicans were just as human as Americans.

Actually, the only thing that kept the most unruly and undisciplined soldiers from open conflict with Mexican civilians was combat or the promise of combat. Shortly after the Agua Nueva atrocity incident, Taylor's troops were to have all the combat they could handle, at the Battle of Buena Vista.

8
The Battle
of Buena Vista

Santa Anna ordered his army north to attack Taylor's depleted forces in mid-February, 1847. When scouts brought Taylor word that they had seen several thousand advancing Mexicans, the American general was surprised but wise enough to realize that his scouts had seen the leading elements of an attacking enemy army.

"Let them come," Taylor said. "Damned if they don't go back a good deal faster than they came."

Nevertheless, Taylor immediately ordered his army to withdraw to a place called Buena Vista, which offered ideal terrain for a defensive stand.

Santa Anna approached Taylor along a road that ran through a deep valley. At Buena Vista the valley became a narrow gorge through which only a single column of men could pass. On either side of this defile there were high, rocky bluffs. Taylor had placed most of his troops on these bluffs, but down in the defile he had set up an artillery battery commanded by Lieutenant Braxton Bragg, backed up by an Indiana regiment of volunteer infantry.

Santa Anna was surprised to find Taylor's forces—there were about 4,500 of them—so firmly established in such an excellent defensive position. When Santa Anna had learned that Taylor had ordered a withdrawal from Agua Nueva, the Mexican general had assumed that the Americans had fled to Saltillo in fear of the far superior Mexican force of more than 15,000. Now, Santa Anna realized, he must meet and defeat the Americans in battle, something he had been hoping to avoid.

On the beautifully clear morning of February 22, Santa Anna sent a force of cavalry toward Taylor's position. When the cavalry reached a point just out of gunshot range, they stopped, and a Mexican officer carrying a white flag rode forward to deliver a demand for surrender. When the demand was read to Taylor, the crusty old Rough and Ready said:

"Tell him to go to hell."

Then, thinking better of his reply, Taylor turned to an aide, Major William Bliss, and said:

"Bliss, put that into Spanish."

Bliss did so, and the reply that was delivered to Santa Anna became:

"I beg leave to say that I decline to accede to your request. If General Santa Anna wants us, he must come and get us."

After the Battle of Buena Vista, the story of Taylor's reply and Bliss's rewording of it was told and re-told in numerous newspaper accounts of the battle, and "Put that into Spanish" became a popular American phrase.

Santa Anna wasted no further time before going into action. He immediately ordered his artillery to begin firing on the ridges on either side of the Buena Vista valley, and then sent forward a probing cavalry attack against the American left flank. By nightfall, however, no decisive action had taken place. That night the Americans slept on their guns, and General Taylor rode Old Whitey back to Saltillo to check on the defenses there, leaving General Wool in charge at Buena Vista. Saltillo was Taylor's main supply source, and he was afraid Santa Anna might circle around the Buena Vista area and attack Saltillo.

The next day, Santa Anna attacked in earnest, sending a powerful force of cavalry and infantry against the American left flank along one of the bluffs. Before Taylor could return from Saltillo, his army was faced with near-disaster. The Mexican attack had sent the American left flank reeling in retreat. But just as Santa Anna was preparing to turn this retreat into a rout, Taylor came galloping up on Old Whitey, accompanied by reinforcements from Saltillo. Taylor's arrival with a sharpshooting regiment of Jefferson Davis's Mississippi Rifles momentarily turned the tide of battle, the rapid and accurate fire from the Mississippians' guns breaking the Mexican charge.

Battle of Buena Vista
PHOTO: SAN JACINTO MUSEUM OF HISTORY

That afternoon, Santa Anna resumed his attack on the American left. This time he intended to smash his way through to the rear of the American line and capture the road to Saltillo. A rainstorm swept over the battlefield in the midst of the attack, but it did not stop the hand-to-hand fighting with knives and bayonets. Eventually the Americans managed to drive the Mexicans back to their original positions.

Late in the afternoon, when the combat lines were restored, Taylor sent several regiments of volunteers —including two from Arkansas—against the Mexicans, but they were stopped in their tracks after suffering fearful casualties. The Mexicans retaliated with yet another cavalry and infantry charge—the most powerful one of the battle—but this time Lieutenant Bragg's artillery battery was moved quickly into position on the bluff from its original location on the valley floor. Taylor told Bragg that the position "must be held at all costs."

Then Taylor asked what kind of shot was being used in the guns, grapeshot or canister.

"Canister," he was told.*

"Good," Taylor said. "Put double the usual load in every gun—and give 'em hell, Bragg."

---

* Canister consisted of a number of metal balls enclosed in a case or cylinder that exploded when fired. It was used for close-range artillery fire. Grapeshot was usually used for long-range artillery fire. It was a cluster of metal balls fastened together by iron rings and resembled a bunch of grapes.

Give 'em hell Bragg and his men did, their first salvo stopping the enemy just a few yards from the muzzles of the cannon. Their second salvo tore great gaping holes in the charging Mexican line. Then, as the Mexicans faltered, Bragg ordered his massed artillery to commence quick-fire salvos, and, in less than an hour, Santa Anna ordered a retreat.

The day's battle had actually been a draw, with the Americans as exhausted as the Mexicans. That night the weary Americans again slept on their guns—this time in the rain. They fully expected a renewal of the enemy attack the following day. But that night Santa Anna had his soldiers keep their campfires burning to hide the retreat of the entire Mexican army to Taylor's former camp at Agua Nueva. Before retreating, however, Santa Anna shrewdly took with him all of the American guns and equipment his men had captured in the course of the battle. Later, placing this captured American equipment on display at San Luis Potosí, he claimed to have defeated the Americans at Buena Vista.

The next day, the Americans, including General Taylor and General Wool, who threw their arms about one another in joy, could scarcely believe their eyes when they saw the empty enemy camp. By now the rain had stopped and a magnificent rainbow shone over the battlefield, as if to symbolize the American victory. The victory had been a costly one, however. Taylor's losses were 272 killed, 387 wounded, and 6 missing. Mexican casualties were at least twice as high, Santa Anna admitting to 591 killed, more than 1,000 wounded, and almost 2,000 missing. Many of the missing Mexicans were deserters.

The Battle of Buena Vista, which ended on February 23, 1847, also ended the U.S. Army's highly successful campaign in northern Mexico. The action now moved to the southern theater, where Scott was engaged in the amphibious landing at Veracruz.

9
Amphibious Landing at Veracruz

The U.S. Navy had taken over the port city of Tampico, Mexico, and nearby Lobos Island without opposition in late November, 1846. When General Scott withdrew troops from General Taylor, Scott had them assemble at Tampico. These were mostly regulars. He also had some regulars, but mostly volunteers, assemble at the mouth of the Brazos River in Texas. The combined force that was to engage in America's first major amphibious landing, at Veracruz, numbered about 14,000 men, half of whom were regulars.

General Scott had decided to use Lobos Island as his main staging area, but his forces were slow to assemble at the mouth of the Brazos and at Tampico. Scott began to be seriously concerned about the success of his mission when a number of his troops at Tampico fell ill with smallpox. He was also as aware as Taylor had been that the *el vómito* season was about to begin, and he was fearful that his entire command might be stricken with the dread yellow fever scourge. Finally, by mid-February, 1847, the two divisions of Scott's army were able to leave Tampico and the mouth of the Brazos and reassemble on Lobos Island. They sailed from there for Veracruz on March 2.

Included among Scott's top command were most of that honor roll of future Civil War heroes—Beauregard, Meade, Johnston, Lee, Jackson, and Grant, among others. All these officers sailed with Scott aboard one of the more than eighty troop transports, and it wasn't until some years after the safe and successful Veracruz landings that observers speculated about what course the Civil War might have taken had Scott's command ship been sunk in Mexican waters.

But the landings on the beaches at Veracruz on March 9 took place virtually without incident. Since Santa Anna and his main Mexican army had just been defeated by General Taylor at Buena Vista in the north, the Mexican army commander at Veracruz, General Juan Morales, had a force of only 4,500 men available to resist the landings. Rather than risk his men in a direct defense of the beaches, Morales decided to keep his army inside the high city walls.

As their landing craft—especially built for this assault—moved through the surf toward the beaches, the American troops could not believe they weren't being fired upon. The first assault troops planted the Amer-

Landing at Veracruz

PHOTO: U.S. ARMY

ican flag on the beaches in the late afternoon. Additional troops soon followed, accompanied by bands playing "The Star-Spangled Banner." By midnight, some 10,000 men were ashore without having suffered a single casualty.

Whatever General Morales's reasons were for not contesting the landings, military historians later agreed that the Mexican commander had made a grave error. For the first several hours of the landings, there were only a few American troops ashore, since the landing craft had to make several trips from the troopships to shore and back again to land the entire assault force. Even token resistance would have seriously delayed the American assault, and a cavalry charge at the precise moment the first assault wave hit the beach would probably have defeated the landings.

Scott and his command had little time for rejoicing, however. The landings had indeed been successful, but the walled city of Veracruz had still to be taken—not to mention the fortress of San Juan de Ulúa. This fortress, which stood in Veracruz harbor, was manned by 1,200 of Morales's crack troops and was regarded as the strongest fortress on the continent. Scott's decision was to lay siege to the city and its harbor fortress.

Within a week, Scott's troops had thrown a seven-mile-long ring around Veracruz, and his artillery began to hammer the city into submission. As the siege lines were established, another incident occurred that might have changed the future course of U.S. history. Future Confederate leaders Pierre Beauregard and Robert E. Lee, while on patrol duty, were almost shot by an American sentry. Neither man was hit, but a bullet from the overeager sentry's gun pierced Lee's uniform.

But the greatest danger to the American army proved to be the yellow fever both Scott and Taylor had feared. Hundreds of soldiers contracted it, and many of them died. The army was never free of *el vómito,* in fact, until the campaign had moved into the highlands near Mexico City.

The American siege of Veracruz continued for several weeks, but the Mexicans gave no sign of surrender. In addition to the several thousand enemy troops inside the city walls, there were some 15,000 civilians, and the casualty toll among them both from shellfire and disease began to mount. Scott regretted having to carry on this warfare against a civilian population, but he saw no other way to solve the problem other than by continued siege.

One of Scott's problems in carrying out a successful siege was the fact that his artillery mortars were too light to fire shells that did much damage against either the city's walls or the walls of the harbor fortress. This problem was solved as far as the city walls were concerned when U.S. Navy Commodore Matthew C. Perry suggested that Scott use several heavy naval guns for bombardment. Interestingly enough, Matthew

Perry's brother, Oliver Hazard Perry, had cooperated in similar fashion with General William Harrison to win the Battle of Lake Erie during the War of 1812.*

Matthew Perry's suggestion to Scott was gladly accepted. Six heavy naval guns and their crews were brought ashore, and their emplacement was supervised by Robert E. Lee. Late in March, Scott sent a formal demand to Morales for the surrender of the city. When it was refused, a four-day bombardment began, not only with cannonballs and mortar shells, but also with Congreve rockets that the Navy made available to the Army. These rockets also dated back to the War of 1812, when they were used in the British bombardment of Fort McHenry which was witnessed by Francis Scott Key and inspired him to write the words to "The Star-Spangled Banner." During the course of the American bombardment of Veracruz, more than half a million pounds of shells were fired into the city, 7,000 mortar rounds being fired by the Army artillery and 2,000 cannonballs being fired from the heavy naval guns.

On March 25, Morales requested that women and children be allowed to evacuate the city. Scott refused the request, demanding complete surrender. Morales then resigned his command to General José Juan Landero, who offered to surrender the next day. On

* See another book in this series, *The War of 1812: America's Second War for Independence.*

Bombardment of Veracruz
PHOTO: SAN JACINTO MUSEUM OF HISTORY

March 29, having stacked their arms, the Mexicans marched out of Veracruz, and Scott's army marched in and raised the Stars and Stripes over the city. Scott named General William Worth military governor, and Scott began to prepare to march on Mexico City.

It was never accurately determined how many civilian casualties there were in the siege of Veracruz, but estimates ran as high as 600 killed and 900 wounded. An equal number of Mexican soldiers were killed. The Americans suffered 13 killed and 55 wounded. Casualties among the defenders of the harbor fortress were relatively light, and its walls were not breached. Since supplies and ammunition never presented a serious problem to the Mexican defenders, critics afterward accused General Morales of cowardice in surrendering.

Before he left Veracruz, General Scott made a valiant effort to prevent any mistreatment of Mexican civilians by American occupation troops. His General Order No. 20 called for the severe punishment of any soldier committing any crime against Mexican civilians, and he called upon every soldier who honored his country and respected himself to help maintain law and order. Scott's words were given added emphasis when one man who disregarded them was publicly hanged.

10
The Capture of Santa Anna's Wooden Leg

The loyal followers of Mexican General Santa Anna often said he had as many lives as a cat. This was true in both a military and political sense, and to some degree in a physical sense as well. The closest he ever came to death in battle was in 1839, when a French warship bombarded Veracruz while Santa Anna was commandant there. At the time, Santa Anna's political fortunes were at a low ebb, but in successfully resisting the attack of the French, who claimed that Mexico owed France vast sums of money, Santa Anna once again became a national hero. In the course of the bombardment, however, the Mexican leader lost a leg. He recovered quickly from this severe injury, but within half a dozen years his fortunes had again fallen. It was then that he was exiled to Cuba.

Santa Anna's military and political fortunes continued to ebb and flow all during the course of Mexico's war with the United States. After his defeat by General Taylor at Buena Vista, his fortunes were again at an extremely low ebb, but Santa Anna hurried back to Mexico City, where he somehow convinced the church to lend him several million dollars, and prevailed upon the Mexican Congress to keep him in power. He was also somehow able to raise a brand-new army of 12,000 men with which to face the advancing General Scott. But following the surrender of Veracruz, Santa Anna and his new army were threatened with a revolt of the Mexican people against his military leadership. The wily Mexican leader met this threat with a proclamation to his people promising to defeat Scott's invasion force at a pass in the mountains called Cerro Gordo. The Mexican people accepted this proclamation. Thus Santa Anna had proved once again that he had as many military and political lives as a cat, by twice returning to life as the nation's top leader within a few weeks after his defeat at Buena Vista and the loss of Veracruz.

Although Scott was eager to escape the fever-ridden lowlands by moving his army into the uplands of the interior, he was not able to do so until early in April. The main reason for delay was a lack of horses, mules, and wagons to transport his 8,500 men and their supplies. When Scott was finally able to move out from Veracruz toward Jalapa, a small town on the road to Mexico City, he found that Santa Anna had chosen his defensive position well.

General Antonio López de Santa Anna
PHOTO: SAN JACINTO MUSEUM OF HISTORY

Santa Anna had been born at Jalapa, and as a boy had become familiar with all of the surrounding countryside. Knowing that Scott with his wagon transport would probably have to use the main national highway that ran from Veracruz through Jalapa to Mexico City, Santa Anna decided to block Scott's advance at Cerro Gordo, where the road threaded its way through a deep canyon surrounded by high cliff walls.

Santa Anna's defensive position was thus very much like Taylor's at Buena Vista. On one side of the road, atop two high points, El Telégrafo ("Telegraph Hill") and La Atalaya, Santa Anna had built breastworks, behind which were stationed most of his men. Here he had also installed heavy-artillery batteries zeroed in on the road below. On the other side of the road he had also stationed troops and a few heavy guns. This side, the Mexican right, Santa Anna did not feel had to be so heavily defended, because the rough terrain was all but impossible to cross, and a river, the Río del Plan, formed a natural barrier at the far right.

When Scott neared Cerro Gordo canyon, some thirty miles from Veracruz, his scouts told him the Mexicans were blocking the way. They also told him a frontal assault down the main road along which they were traveling would be suicide. Scott then sent additional scouts forward, and on the basis of their reports he decided that an attack on the Mexican right was also impossible. During the course of their reconnaissance, however, one of Scott's scouts, Robert E. Lee, had discovered a path that led around the Mexican left to La Atalaya hill. Scott immediately decided upon his plan of attack. He would feint with an attack on the right, but send his main attack along the path to the left. This main thrust would completely encircle the Mexican position on the left, move to the rear of Santa Anna's forces, and capture the main road that led to Jalapa.

First of all, however, the path Lee had discovered would have to be cleared and widened so it would allow not only infantry troops but also artillery to pass along it. This feat was performed, mostly by night, without alerting the Mexican army. Then, on the morning of April 17, an infantry division under General David Twiggs attacked and captured La Atalaya before the Mexicans were fully aware of what was happening. Santa Anna immediately sent reinforcements to support his left flank, and Scott reinforced Twiggs, hoping for a break in the Mexican lines.

The following morning, a clear, cool Sunday, began with an artillery duel between the opposed armies, and then Scott sent in his feint on the right, led by General Gideon Pillow. Pillow was not a military man, but he was the former peacetime law partner of President Polk, who had appointed him brigadier general. Pillow completely mismanaged his part of the attack, failing to launch it on time, neglecting to give attack orders to certain regiments, and, finally, suffering a bullet wound in his arm before appointing an aide to assume command in case he became a casualty.

Fortunately, the attack on the left against El Telégrafo went forward despite Pillow's floundering feint on the right. After capturing La Atalaya, Twiggs had placed artillery there and zeroed in on El Telégrafo. These guns covered Colonel William S. Harney's men as they attacked up the steep slopes of El Telégrafo, using their swords and guns as walking sticks to help them climb to the top. Once on the summit, Harney's troops engaged the Mexican defenders in a fierce, hand-to-hand struggle, finally driving the enemy from their position.

Meanwhile, Scott had sent two of Twiggs's other brigades around the base of El Telégrafo. These troops managed to fight their way to the Jalapa road, which they captured by midmorning. Thus, as the Mexicans fled down El Telégrafo, their retreat along the main road was cut off. They attempted to escape in all directions into the surrounding mountains. Many were taken prisoner, and Santa Anna himself barely escaped capture.

The Sunday battle of Cerro Gordo had lasted only three hours. After it was over, Scott counted 200 Mexican officers and about 3,000 enlisted men as prisoners. No other Mexican casualty figures were available because of the disorganization of Santa Anna's command. In addition to these prisoners and the shattering of yet another of Santa Anna's armies, Scott had captured

*Santa Anna's Wooden Leg.
At the Battle of Cerro
Gordo, members of the
Fourth Regiment of
Illinois volunteers
captured a disabled coach
from which General
Santa Anna had unhitched
a horse to make good his
escape. Inside the coach
they found a roasted
chicken and Santa Anna's
wooden leg. They ate the
chicken and brought the
wooden leg back to
Illinois as a souvenir.*

PHOTO: ILLINOIS STATE
HISTORICAL LIBRARY

huge stores of ammunition, 43 cannon, 4,000 muskets, food, and other supplies. American casualties numbered 63 killed and 368 wounded.

On the following day, the American army moved on to Jalapa, where they settled down to enjoy their victory at Cerro Gordo and congratulate themselves on all of the prize booty captured from the Mexicans. Included among their prizes was General Santa Anna's personal war chest, containing more than $20,000 in gold. Biggest prize of all, however, was Santa Anna's wooden leg. A regiment of Illinois volunteers had captured the leg, which they managed to keep all through the remainder of the war, finally bringing it back with them to their home state when they were mustered out of service. For many years afterward, Santa Anna's wooden leg was kept on display at Springfield, Illinois, in the state capitol. Soon after the story of the victorious battle of Cerro Gordo was told in the American press, miniature "Santa Anna wooden legs" became popular as souvenirs sold throughout the United States.

11
A Jar of Guava Jelly

Mexico City, capital of Mexico and key to the control of the entire country, was just 170 miles from Scott and his American forces at Jalapa. As far as Scott knew, there were no enemy forces between him and the nation's capital. With this glittering prize virtually within his grasp, Scott was tempted to reach out and seize it. But before ordering his army forward along the national highway, Scott had numerous problems to solve.

His first problem was one of obtaining essential supplies, food for his troops and forage for his horses and mules. He had expected to obtain these at Jalapa, but here he was disappointed. While the Mexican civilians seemed friendly enough, they had little food or forage to offer. Consequently, supplies had to be brought in from Veracruz, and most of Scott's cavalry had to be used to protect the wagon trains moving inland from the coast against the many Mexican guerrillas.

An equally important problem was manpower. Poor food and many weeks in the lowlands had resulted in widespread illness throughout the American Army. By late May, more than 3,000 of Scott's troops were hospitalized because of wounds or fever. Most serious of all, however, was the fact that the terms of enlistment of many of Scott's volunteer regiments were about to expire. He and his officers made some effort to persuade these volunteers to reenlist for the duration of the war, but these efforts met with little success. Curiously, men whose enlisted terms were almost up felt little or no reluctance about simply walking away from their fellow soldiers, with whom they had shared daily hardships and the dangers of combat all during the campaign. The fact that few of them had received any pay may have influenced their decision to leave for home. Within a matter of weeks, Scott's army was reduced to fewer than 6,000 effective officers and enlisted men.

Early in May, despite the condition of his command, Scott began a cautious advance toward the city of Puebla. By this time, Santa Anna had regrouped some of his scattered army and made a brief defensive stand at Puebla, a city of some 80,000 people and second in size only to the nation's capital. When Santa Anna's defensive stand was broken by an advance party of Americans led by General Worth, the Mexican commander hastily retreated toward Mexico City. Scott's little army, virtually isolated in the heart of an enemy country, now settled down for ten long weeks, awaiting supplies, reinforcements, and the outcome of negotiations for peace that had again been set in motion by the busy President Polk.

Polk had not forgotten General Taylor's agreement to a lengthy armistice after Taylor had taken Monterrey. Consequently, Polk thought military men had no business arranging any kind of armistice for the purpose of discussing peace terms with either an enemy military or civilian government. Polk was also still keenly aware of the political situation in the United States. Both Taylor and Scott were now being widely talked about as presidential candidates by the Whig political party. If Polk could negotiate a peace before Scott took Mexico City, such a feat would bring great credit to Polk's Democratic party. Even if Polk himself was not renominated for the presidency, he did want a say in picking his party's candidate.

With all of these things in mind, Polk selected a civilian Democrat, Nicholas P. Trist, who was something of a secondary official in the State Department, to go to Mexico, join up with Scott's forces, and attempt to engage in peace negotiations with the Mexican government—namely, General Santa Anna. Polk was still convinced that Santa Anna could be bought off and Mexico delivered into U.S. hands without further bloodshed. To this end, Polk had ramrodded through Congress an appropriation of up to $3,000,000 to be used as "extraordinary expenses" to end the war. Beyond that, Trist was authorized to state that the American government would pay up to $30,000,000 for a satisfactory peace settlement, which would include the Mexican acceptance of all boundary claims made by the United States.

When he first learned that a civilian was to be attached to his army as a peace commissioner, General Scott was, of course, furious. He was even more furious when he was told by Secretary of War Marcy that Trist was authorized to declare a truce in order to discuss peace terms with the Mexicans. Scott immediately accused Marcy of "trying to degrade me by requiring that the commander of this army shall defer to the chief clerk of the State Department in deciding the question of continuing or discontinuing the hostilities."

On his part, Trist did not improve matters by failing to meet with Scott after landing at Veracruz. Instead, he sent Scott a letter announcing his arrival, stating the command authority that had been given to him by President Polk, and then awaited Scott's invitation to his headquarters at Puebla.

No such invitation came because the furious Scott had no intention of meeting with Trist. Trist was not wholly surprised, since before leaving Washington he had been told by Polk that the president's old law partner, General Pillow, was actually the man to trust, not Scott.

Scott's triumphant entrance into the Mexican capital

Scott and Trist did continue to exchange letters, and Scott's rage continued to grow. In one letter, Scott even suggested to Trist that he should have come to Mexico armed with a guillotine so he could chop off the heads of leaders as had been done in the French Revolution.

In a final outburst, Scott wrote to Secretary of War Marcy: "Considering the many cruel disappointments and mortifications I have been made to feel since I left Washington, and the total lack of support and sympathy on the part of the War Department which I have so long experienced, I beg leave to be recalled."

Fortunately, Marcy chose to ignore what amounted to Scott's resignation.

By mid-June, with Scott and Trist both in Puebla but still not speaking to one another, Trist decided to go outside Army channels and contact the Mexican government directly to attempt peace negotiations. Trist's contact in Mexico City was the British foreign minister there, Edward Thornton. Thornton came to Puebla and told Trist that the Mexican government was willing to negotiate but all of the Mexican officials were afraid to do so. Their fear was caused by a law that the Mexican Congress had just passed, making anyone who discussed peace terms with any American guilty of treason and liable to be shot. Thornton indicated, however, that Santa Anna might be persuaded to negotiate secretly.

While in Puebla, Thornton was also successful in

getting Trist to meet with Scott and relay Thornton's report to the commanding general. After this meeting, the two Americans were much more friendly toward one another. Then, early in July, Trist fell ill. Learning of Trist's illness, Scott sent him a friendly note, accompanied by a jar of the general's favorite guava jelly. From that moment on, Scott and Trist were fast friends.

When Trist recovered, he opened secret negotiations with General Santa Anna, even keeping them secret from President Polk. Santa Anna's terms were put quite bluntly. First of all, Santa Anna was to be given $10,000 as an initial payment. Next, Scott's army was to leave Puebla and march on Mexico City, and there stage a token attack on the capital. This would give Santa Anna an excuse for surrendering Mexico City, following which Santa Anna would be given $1,000,000.

Both Trist and Scott thought Santa Anna's offer was a good one, but they were somewhat concerned about the accusations of bribery that might be made against them if the deal fell through. Like Polk, however, both Trist and Scott were aware of how their political fortunes might be improved if they succeeded in buying peace without further bloodshed. By this time, even Trist was seeing himself as the next presidential candidate.

But before going ahead with any further arrangements, Scott discussed the proposed deal with his senior officers, Generals John Quitman, Gideon Pillow, James Shields, George Cadwalader, and David Twiggs. Pillow, Polk's friend, favored the deal. Twiggs would not discuss it, and the other three officers mildly opposed it, pointing out that it was bribery that could prove embarrassing.

"Nonsense," Scott said. "The 'corrupt offer,' if it is indeed corrupt, came from a man who is already corrupted. Santa Anna volunteered to put himself on the auction block." Scott then went on to point out that similar deals had been made with various American Indian tribes in taking over their lands.

It was clear that Scott had already made up his mind, but the next question was where to get the down payment of $10,000 without alerting Washington. Scott solved this by taking the money out of his secret service fund.

Within a few days, Trist made arrangements to deliver the money. Then he and Scott sat back and awaited further word from Santa Anna. When word finally came, it was to the effect that Santa Anna would be threatened with a revolution and his life would be in danger if he even suggested further negotiations to the Mexican people.

Scott now realized he had not only made a donation in dollars to Santa Anna's war chest, but he had also donated precious time during which the Mexican leader could strengthen the defenses of Mexico City. Wisely, if somewhat belatedly, Scott returned to conducting a military conquest of the Mexican capital rather than a diplomatic one. Fortunately, he had just received word that his army's strength was to be greatly increased by the prospective arrival of six or eight new divisions under Generals William O. Butler and Franklin Pierce. The advance toward Mexico City began on August 5, 1847.

12
The Twin Battles of Contreras and Churubusco

When Scott decided to leave Puebla and advance on Mexico City, he had about 10,000 men in his army. Santa Anna, on the other hand, had between 25,000 and 30,000 troops with which to defend the nation's capital, a city of 200,000 people. Because he was outnumbered by about three to one, Scott could leave only a token force behind him to defend Puebla. He had absolutely no men to spare to fight off the Mexican guerrillas who continued to threaten the primary supply route between his main army and Veracruz. Consequently, Scott made a daring decision. He would make no attempt to keep his supply route open. Instead, he would abandon all contact with the coast and, as he wrote Secretary Marcy, make his "brave little army a self-sustaining machine."

Scott's daring decision struck some observers as

foolhardy. No less famous a military hero than the Duke of Wellington, Great Britain's "Iron Duke," who had defeated Napoleon at the Battle of Waterloo, commented:

"Scott is lost. He cannot capture the city, and he cannot fall back upon his base."

Nevertheless, Scott set out, and in about a week his army had made its way up onto the great plateau on which Mexico City was situated. Here they encountered the first of the Mexican defenses.

Mexico City was ideally situated for defensive purposes, and Santa Anna had taken full advantage of every natural feature in disposing his forces. Between Scott's approaching army and the Mexican capital lay three large lakes, Lake Chalco, Lake Xochimilco, and Lake Texcoco. There was also a large dry bed of lava called the Pedregal. This rocky area was considered completely impassable, one Mexican general observing that "not even a bird could get through the Pedregal."

Surrounding these lakes and the lava beds were a series of swampy marshlands that were also impassable. Actually, the only available routes to the city's gates seemed to be across a series of giant elevated causeways, where Santa Anna had concentrated most of his defensive forces. These forces were divided into three armies, one inside the city itself, one to the south, and one to the north. On the main national road along which Scott was advancing, Santa Anna had established what was probably his strongest defensive point

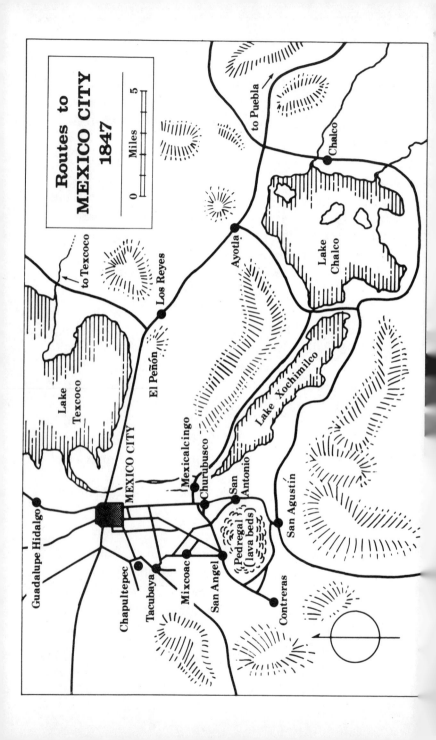

at a hill called El Peñón, because it was here he expected Scott to make his strongest assault.

Scott's forces were divided into four separate units under Generals Pillow, Quitman, Twiggs, and Worth. When the first Mexican defenses were encountered, Scott ordered the four divisions to remain in place while he sent his scouts forward to assess the situation. The news they brought back was not good. An attack on the heavily fortified El Peñón seemed out of the question, since Santa Anna had most of his artillery massed there, and any frontal assault would result in unacceptable losses.

Scott had just about made up his mind to attack to the north, at a point called Mexicalcingo, when a scout from General Worth's division reported that he had discovered a road that led south of Lakes Chalco and Xochimilco to the town of San Agustín (today's Tlalpán). Not only was this road suitable for infantry, cavalry, wagons, and artillery, but it circled below a low mountain range that would block off any enemy fire from El Peñón.

Without hesitation, Scott ordered his army to move out, and by mid-August all of his men were in San Agustín without having suffered a casualty. This brilliant flanking move put Scott in a position where he could move directly against Mexico City. It also made the outflanked defenses on El Peñón completely useless, since Scott was now well beyond the range of the artillery stationed there. Hastily, Santa Anna moved the El Peñón guns to the town of San Antonio in an attempt to block Scott's approach.

Scott sent General Worth's division toward San Antonio, but at the same time he asked Captain Robert E. Lee to find a way through the lava beds of the Pedregal. Lee returned to report that he and Lieutenant Beauregard had found a path through the lava beds, but they had also sighted a strong Mexican force at the far edge of the Pedregal at the town of Contreras. These troops were commanded by General Gabriel Valencia.

Despite the presence of Valencia's troops, Scott put Lee in charge of several hundred men to turn the Pedregal path into a road suitable for wagons and artillery to use. This superhuman feat was accomplished in twenty-four hours, and on the night of August 19, Scott moved his army across the lava beds. The next morning, the Americans faced the startled Valencia.

When Santa Anna, who was at San Antonio, learned that Scott had crossed the Pedregal, he realized that he was about to be outflanked again. Santa Anna immediately sent word to Valencia to retreat from his position at Contreras at the edge of the lava beds and join Santa Anna at San Antonio. Valencia bluntly refused his commanding officer's order. Valencia thought he could defeat Scott and thus gain a hero's role that would rival Santa Anna's.

Scott had a small part of his force attack Valencia from the front, but he sent his main force around to

Capture of a Mexican general at Contreras
PHOTO: U.S. ARMY

Valencia's rear. Valencia's men were in fixed positions, ready to defend against a frontal assault, when they were suddenly set upon from the rear. The Mexican artillerymen tried in vain to turn their guns around, but they were overrun before they could do so. In a matter of moments, the artillerymen broke and ran, followed by the fleeing infantry, many of whom were trampled and killed by the wildly retreating Mexican cavalry. In an unbelievable seventeen minutes, the Battle of Contreras had ended, leaving behind 700 Mexican dead and wounded, 800 prisoners (including several generals), and a wealth of supplies, weapons, and equipment—including much invaluable artillery and ammunition. The Americans had 60 killed and wounded. General Valencia had managed to escape, but the angry Santa Anna ordered Valencia to be shot on sight. Santa Anna also ordered a retreat from San Antonio, which was now outflanked, to Churubusco, where defenses were to be established along the Churubusco River.

Among the defending forces at Churubusco were a number of American soldiers who had deserted from the U.S. Army. These were mostly men who had been, or were about to be, convicted of court-martial offenses committed during the previous year. They had chosen to desert and join the enemy ranks rather than face severe punishment by the American army. Santa Anna had formed them into a separate unit, called the San Patricio Battalion. Santa Anna knew that the San

Patricio deserters would fight without quarter against their former comrades in arms because they faced certain execution for desertion if they were captured.

Santa Anna stationed most of his defensive forces along the Churubusco River. But inside the town, in the Convent of San Mateo, he stationed the San Patricio Battalion, whose members fought, as Ulysses Grant later said, "like men with nooses around their necks."

Scott's forces were weary from the earlier fighting and continued marching, but they went into action immediately and by mid-afternoon had carried the town, driving Santa Anna's defenders before them. The fiercest fighting occurred at the Convent of San Mateo, where the Mexicans tried several times to raise flags of surrender, but every time they did so, American deserters hauled down the surrender flags. When they ran out of ammunition, the men of the San Patricio Battalion resorted to using their guns as clubs, but they, too, were finally forced to surrender. By the time the fighting ended, there were only eighty American deserters left alive. Most of these men were hanged during the following weeks. Those who were not hanged had the letter D branded on their cheeks. In an incredible display of belated loyalty, a number of the condemned men, who were waiting on the backs of flatbed wagons to be hanged, sent up cheers when the American flag was raised on a nearby building to indicate an American victory. When they had finished cheering, the wagons were pulled away and the victims were left to dangle at the ends of nooses strung over nearby cottonwood trees.

General Scott's victorious but isolated U.S. Army was now within rifle shot of the gates of Mexico City. It is possible that if Scott had decided to occupy the capital immediately he could have done so, but his army had suffered almost 1,000 casualties in the twin battles of Contreras and Churubusco—most of them occurring in the latter fight on August 20.

Instead of mounting an assault, Scott sent in a demand for surrender. Santa Anna countered with a request for an armistice, telling Scott that if the Americans continued fighting, the Mexican government officials might all leave the city and Scott would have no one with whom to work out peace terms. After a certain amount of negotiation, Scott once again accepted the wily Mexican commander's bait. He agreed to the armistice and told Trist to try to work out peace terms with Santa Anna and the other Mexican government officials.

Santa Anna was, of course, grateful for the rest. His army had suffered several times as many casualties as the U.S. Army, and a rest was needed to restore the all-but-shattered Mexican soldiers' morale.

The truce lasted two weeks. Then Santa Anna told Trist that the American peace terms were unacceptable. On September 7, Scott prepared to make his final assault upon the city.

13
"God Is a Yankee"

The key defense point at the outer edge of Mexico City was Chapultepec Castle, a centuries-old fortress originally built by the Spanish. Set on a high hill, Chapultepec was being used as a military training academy at the time of the Mexican War. As Scott approached the city, most of the teenaged cadets were removed from the academy and sent to places of safety. But about 100 of them insisted upon remaining as part of the 8,000-man Chapultepec defense force.

A second bastion of defense was the Molino del Rey—or King's Mill. During the brief armistice, Scott's intelligence staff told the general that church bells were being melted down and forged into cannons at the King's Mill. Scott fell victim to this faulty intelligence report, which was probably planted by Santa Anna. The American general should, of course, have realized that any such major foundry operation would have used up far more time than the Mexicans had to spare. In any event, Scott decided to attack the King's Mill first, and then assault Chapultepec Castle.

General Worth, with about 3,200 men—almost half of Scott's entire effective army—was assigned the role of leading the attack on the King's Mill. Worth sent his first wave of attackers against the left side of the Mexican line. This proved to be the strongest part of the enemy's defenses, and the Americans were beaten back. The Mexicans then counterattacked but were repulsed. Worth then ordered a second charge, which broke the Mexican left flank. But a third thrust at the center of the enemy position, against a heavily fortified building called the Casa Mata, resulted in large American troop losses with very little gain in ground. The Casa Mata was finally destroyed by American artillery fire. On the Mexican right, a cavalry charge was sent in by Worth, and the charge shattered and rolled back the enemy line. Within an hour and a half, the Battle of the King's Mill ended in an American victory.

But it was an empty victory. Worth had lost more than 700 men, a fact that caused Ulysses Grant to write in his diary: "A few more such victories and our army will be destroyed."

Once again the Mexican casualty toll was far higher than the American—700 enemy prisoners were taken, and 1,500 of the enemy were dead or wounded. But little else had been gained. No recently made cannons were found, nor even any church bells, melted down or intact.

However, during the course of some of the day's most severe fighting, the Mexican defenders had cut the throats of a number of wounded Americans. Scott's men vowed they would take no prisoners in the assault on Chapultepec Castle.

The Battle of the King's Mill ended on September 8, and the Battle of Chapultepec began on September 13. Santa Anna took personal charge of the Mexican forces, realizing that the loss of this battle would probably mean the loss of the war.

Twenty-four hours before the first assault wave rolled in against Chapultepec, the Americans began a daylong bombardment. Then, at dawn on September 13, Pillow's, Quitman's, and Worth's divisions attacked from three different directions—south, southeast, and west. Twiggs's division was sent on a diversionary movement south of the city.

Pillow's division was the first to reach the castle's outer walls, but then it was discovered that Pillow or his aides had neglected to bring along scaling ladders. While Pillow and his men cowered beneath the stone walls, under withering enemy fire, and awaited the delivery of the scaling ladders, Pillow was slightly wounded. When the ladders did arrive, Pillow's men swarmed over the walls without their commander, and the men from Worth's division soon followed.

Fierce, hand-to-hand fighting took place within the castle. Among the bravest of the defenders were the teenaged Mexican military cadets. Half a dozen died,

Cavalry charge at Chapultepec
PHOTO: U.S. ARMY

122

and one of these casualties, a boy named Agustín Melgar, dueled singlehanded against several dismounted American cavalrymen before he was killed by infantrymen wielding bayonets. This gallant stand by the Chapultepec cadets quickly became part of Mexican patriotic folklore, the story of their bravery being told and retold under the title *"Los Niños Heroicos"* ("The Heroic Children").

It was not Santa Anna but a General Nicolás Bravo who surrendered to General Scott. Although Santa Anna had taken personal charge of the Mexican forces at the battle's beginning, he was among those who managed to escape when the tide turned against them. As the Americans lowered the green, red, and white Mexican tricolor flag and raised the red, white, and blue Stars and Stripes over the castle, Santa Anna and an aide viewed the event from a ridge a safe distance from the final fighting. Watching the American flag reach the top of the staff and then begin to flutter in the mid-morning breeze, Santa Anna said to his aide:

"If we planted our artillery batteries in hell, I think the damned Yankees would take them from us." Then he added, in a tone of defeat: "I think God himself is a Yankee."

There now began a race for control of the whole of Mexico City. Scott began to bombard the center of the city, and his men moved forward through the main gates and down the main streets. But here, as at Monterrey, they had to leave the roadways where they were perfect targets and resort to burrowing their way through the walls of the adobe houses, driving the Mexicans before them.

By nightfall on September 13, the Americans were winning the Battle of Mexico City, but they had lost almost 1,000 men and were on the verge of collapse. Unknown to them, however, Santa Anna was about to solve their problems for them. That night, as the Americans tried to sleep and avoid thinking about a street-to-street and house-to-house struggle for the city on the following day, Santa Anna gathered his remaining forces and stole out of the city. But, before leaving, he released all of the criminals imprisoned in the city's jails, hoping they would fight some sort of guerrilla warfare against Scott.

One of the most important buildings within Mexico City was the National Palace, former home of the Montezuma emperors. The next morning, with General Quitman's division in the lead, the Americans struck out toward the National Palace, realizing that its capture would probably deal a death blow to Mexican morale, both military and civilian.

Quitman and his men were startled to run into almost no opposition. Quickly, they took over the National Palace—or Citadel, as it was also called—and a Marine lieutenant, A. S. Nicholson, raced to the roof, lowered the Mexican flag, and raised the American flag. It was on this incident that the United States

American troops enter Mexico City
PHOTO: SAN JACINTO MUSEUM OF HISTORY

Marines later based the opening of the Marine Corps hymn:

From the Halls of Montezuma,
To the shores of Tripoli.

A short time later, Mexican government officials advanced under a flag of truce and asked for terms for the surrender of the city. Scott told them there were no terms except unconditional surrender, since the city was at his mercy. He did promise to deal in a civilized manner with the civilian population and to treat all military prisoners as prisoners of war subject to parole—without their weapons. The Mexican officials agreed, and Scott named Quitman military governor of the city.

Quitman's first job was rounding up the several thousand criminals whom Santa Anna had released from their jail cells and who were now plundering the city. This task was quickly accomplished, but there remained the final problem of drawing up a peace treaty and getting it accepted by the government officials of the two warring nations. This was not accomplished until the spring of the following year, 1848. And before then both Scott and Trist would be relieved of their duties and recalled to Washington by an ungrateful President Polk.

14
The Treaty of
Guadalupe Hidalgo

When Great Britain's Duke of Wellington heard of Scott's capture of Mexico City, he retracted his earlier comment criticizing the American commander for cutting his army off from its supply base. Now the Iron Duke said:

"Scott's campaign was unsurpassed in military annals. He is the greatest living soldier."

Most historians have agreed that on the battlefield Scott was the best American general between the American Revolution and the Civil War. His entire campaign from the amphibious landing at Veracruz to the capture of Mexico City, and especially his brilliant flanking movements around Santa Anna outside the Mexican capital, was a military masterpiece. Scott's bold daring has, in fact, been favorably compared with General Douglas MacArthur and his amphibious landing at Inchon in Korea and the recapture of the capital city of Seoul in the Korean War.*

Like MacArthur, however, Scott was not at his best when it came to dealing with civilian members of his nation's government—especially the U.S. president. The thought never occurred to either general that he could be wrong, nor did either general fully accept the fact that the president was also commander in chief of all military services and that, right or wrong, the president held the final authority. In the end, these oversights led to the recall of both generals, Scott by President Polk, and MacArthur by President Harry S Truman.

Shortly after the American military government was established in Mexico City, stories began to circulate in Washington giving credit for the victorious campaign to both Generals Pillow and Worth and belittling Scott's role. Scott blamed his two subordinates for circulating these stories—many of which were printed in U.S. newspapers—and had Pillow and Worth placed under arrest for insubordination. This naturally angered President Polk—especially since one of the men arrested was his friend Pillow—and Polk not only ordered Worth's and Pillow's immediate release but also ordered that General Scott's conduct of the campaign be investigated.

* See another book in this series, *The United States in the Korean War: Defending Freedom's Frontier.*

At this point, Polk learned of Scott's and Trist's earlier plan to attempt to buy peace by bribing Santa Anna with the initial $10,000 and the promise of an additional $1,000,000 if a peace treaty could be achieved. Polk went into a rage—at least in part unjustified, since he himself had originally sent Trist to Mexico with a similar scheme in mind—and announced that Scott would be recalled. There was some debate as to who would replace Scott, but on January 13, 1848, Polk selected General William O. Butler, who—to no one's surprise—was a member of Polk's Democratic party.

Scott did not return to the United States, however, until the late spring of 1848, so he was free to consult with Trist in Trist's efforts to obtain a peace treaty. When Scott reached New York, no bands played and no celebrations were held in his honor. Fortunately, the old general was to be heard from again, both in 1852, when he was the Whig candidate for the presidency—he was defeated by his fellow Mexican War general, Franklin Pierce—and in 1861, at the outbreak of the Civil War.

Meanwhile, Peace Commissioner Trist, who was also out of favor with Polk, was nonetheless trying his best to negotiate with the Mexican government officials. Trist's main problem was the fact that, although their country was being run by an American military government, the Mexicans refused to accept the fact that they had been defeated. This understandable national pride was, for a time, aided by the fact that General Santa Anna and other Mexican military leaders had gathered together enough scattered troops to engage in guerrilla-like military action throughout the countryside.

As the diplomatic stalemate continued, the American troops settled down for what appeared would be lengthy service as an army of occupation. Finally, on October 6, 1847, Polk ordered that Trist be recalled. This order took a month and a half to reach Trist, and when it did arrive, Trist decided to ignore it because he still thought he could succeed in obtaining a peace treaty—this time with a new Mexican president, Pedro Anaya, who had just come to power.

Immediately after he was driven out of Mexico City, Santa Anna rallied the remnants of his army and decided to attack the token force Scott had left behind him at Puebla. This attack was beaten off by the American garrison there, whereupon Santa Anna resigned his presidency. But the acting Mexican government would not let matters rest there. Santa Anna was ordered to stand ready for a court-martial and explain his conduct of the war. A short time later, he was again banished from the country—this time to Jamaica. Amazingly, within a few years the disaster-prone Santa Anna would again be returned to the Mexican presidency, and yet again be exiled. Finally, in his eighties, he would creep home to die, lonely and unknown, in his beloved native land.

President James K. Polk

131

Trist's optimism over obtaining a peace treaty by working with the new Mexican president proved to be unfounded. Nevertheless, Trist persisted with the negotiations, despite President Polk's violent reaction to his staying on in Mexico when he had been ordered home. A seventy-page letter which Trist wrote Polk explaining his action did nothing to calm Polk's anger. The president's kindest words were, "I have never in my life felt so indignant."

Nevertheless, Polk now decided to let Trist stay on in Mexico as a peace negotiator—perhaps because he had little choice in the matter—but announced that he would not officially endorse any treaty Trist might obtain until after such a treaty had arrived in Washington and its terms had been fully agreed to by the presidential cabinet and himself. Thus Trist, as an unauthorized agent, continued to consult with what amounted to an unauthorized government for a treaty which no one was sure would be authorized by the U.S. Senate once it was obtained.

Finally, after long months of negotiation, Trist did obtain what he regarded as a satisfactory peace treaty, which was signed by Mexican government officials at Guadalupe Hidalgo on February 2, 1848. This treaty was, in turn, ratified by the U.S. Senate on March 10, and by the Mexican government on March 25.

While the Senate was debating ratification of the treaty, Congressman John Quincy Adams, former senator and sixth U.S. president, suffered a stroke on the floor of the House of Representatives and died three days later, February 23, 1848. He was eighty-one and had served in the House for seventeen years. Once he had been asked if he thought it was beneath the dignity of a former senator and president to serve as a representative. "No person can be degraded serving the people," Adams had said. His last words on his deathbed were: "Thank the officers of the House. This is the last of earth. I am content." The circumstances of Congressman Adams's death inspired his friends in the House's sister chamber, the Senate, to bring peace to the nation by ratifying the treaty.

By the terms of the Treaty of Guadalupe Hidalgo, Mexico recognized the Rio Grande River as the boundary between the United States and Mexico, and ceded New Mexico and California to the United States. The United States, in turn, agreed to pay Mexico $15,000,000. There were some congressmen who wanted to annex the whole of Mexico, but Polk stood firm against this move. As it was, the area acquired by the United States amounted to more than half a million square miles of territory. In monetary cost this amounted to less than 50 cents an acre.

Although President Polk had finally accepted Trist's treaty efforts—again, perhaps, because he had little or no choice—Polk had his final revenge. Trist was dismissed from the State Department, and the president refused to authorize payment of Trist's expenses while he was in Mexico. Trist finally received the money due him many years later and long after Polk was out of office.

The last American troops left Mexico City on June 12, 1848. By the first week in August, the last troop-ship had sailed from Veracruz for the United States. The cost of the victory in human terms rather than in dollars and cents had been high, for behind them the American Army had left almost 13,000 dead, most of whom had died from disease. Four thousand men had suffered wounds, while 9,500 men, mostly volunteers, had previously been discharged for varying kinds of disabilities.

It is interesting to note that 50 percent of the men wounded in the Mexican War died, while in the Vietnam conflict only 2.5 percent of those wounded died. It is also interesting to note that there were more than 9,000 deserters during the Mexican War, a far greater ratio per total troop strength than in the Vietnam conflict, a war that became notorious for the number of deserters and draft evaders. Again, most of the deserters in the Mexican War were from the volunteer ranks. Most of these men were recent immigrants to the United States and scarcely regarded the nation as their homeland. Thus it was even more ironic that the San Patricio Battalion captives had cheered the raising of the American flag shortly before they were hanged.

15
Prelude to the Civil War

While the Mexican War solved few problems beyond finally determining the boundary lines of the continental United States (except for Alaska), it did add fuel to the fire that would soon threaten to destroy the young American republic in the raging conflagration of a civil war. This fuel came in the form of new territory and the debate over whether slavery should be allowed in this new land.

The slavery question had been debated endlessly since the days of the Founding Fathers, and the problem was no closer to solution at the end of the Mexican War than it had been at its start. If anything, the problem had now become so complex that armed civil strife seemed inevitable. Compromise had already been tried—and with no little success—in the form of the Missouri Compromise, which attempted to maintain a balance between free states and slave states. But now the delicate balance was about to be upset by the new territory acquired in the Mexican War.

Actually, the new territory was not economically suitable for slavery, since much of it was dry, barren, and not readily adaptable for use in planting and harvesting large field crops like cotton. But this point was seldom debated. What was debated, and finally fought over, was whether or not slavery should be allowed in the area. While the territory was still a part of Mexico, the ugly problem of slavery did not rear its head, since the Mexicans did not believe in it.

Early in the Mexican War a serious attempt was made to ban slavery from any territory acquired during the course of the war. This came in the form of the so-called Wilmot Proviso. When President Polk tried to work out his original deal with Santa Anna, offering him a "safe-conduct" passage from Havana to Mexico, plus $2,000,000 for any territory acquired from Mexico, Polk said he was simply following the procedure established by President Thomas Jefferson when he bought the Louisiana Territory from France. But members of the House of Representatives violently objected. This was no Louisiana Purchase, they said, but an out-and-out attempt to extend the slavery area of the United States by bribing a Mexican official.

Congressman David Wilmot tried to meet this objection by offering an amendment to the appropriations bill for $2,000,000 that stated that slavery would not be allowed in any territory acquired from Mexico.

The House adopted this amendment, which Polk called "mischievous and foolish," but it was rejected by the Senate, led by its majority of Southern senators. The amendment continued to be attached to numerous bills, but always unsuccessfully. David Wilmot, whose proviso was used as a basis for debate over the slavery issue until slavery was banned from the United States in 1862 during the Civil War, was also one of the founders of the Republican party in 1854.

There were a number of "firsts" in the Mexican War. For the first time, an American military expeditionary force was sent overseas by troopship to take part in an amphibious landing on foreign shores. During the War of 1812 there were minor amphibious landings on the Great Lakes, but the start of the Veracruz–Mexico City expedition included the first major amphibious landing by U.S. troops. And at the end of the Mexican War, the U.S. Army, for the first time in its march along the road of Manifest Destiny, was called upon to establish a military government over a conquered nation.

Bibliography

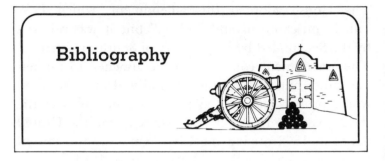

Army, Department of the, *American Military History,* Washington, D.C., 1959.

Bauer, K. Jack, *The Mexican War,* Macmillan Publishing Co., Inc., New York, 1974.

Berky, Andrew S., and Shenton, James P., editors, *The Historians' History of the United States,* G. P. Putnam's Sons, New York, 1966.

Downey, Fairfax, *Sound of the Guns,* David McKay Co., Inc., New York, 1955–56.

Esposito, Colonel Vincent J., editor, *The West Point Atlas of American Wars,* Vol. I, Frederick A. Praeger Publishers, New York, 1959.

Gabriel, Ralph Henry, editor, *The Pageant of America,* Vol. II, Yale University Press, New Haven, 1927.

Grant, U. S., *Personal Memoirs,* The World Publishing Co., Cleveland and New York, 1952.

Henry, Robert Selph, *The Story of the Mexican War,* The Bobbs-Merrill Co., Inc., Indianapolis and New York, 1950.

Leckie, Robert, *The Wars of America,* Harper & Row, Publishers, New York, 1968.

Lewis, Lloyd, *Captain Sam Grant,* Little, Brown & Co., Boston, 1950.

Livingston-Little, D. E., editor, *The Mexican War Diary of Thomas D. Tennery,* University of Oklahoma Press, Norman, 1970.

Lord, Walter, *A Time to Stand,* Harper & Brothers, New York, 1961.

Nevins, Allan, *Ordeal of the Union: Fruits of Manifest Destiny,* Vol. I, Charles Scribner's Sons, New York, 1947.

Scott, Winfield, *Memoirs,* Sheldon & Co., New York, 1864.

Singletary, Otis A., *The Mexican War,* University of Chicago Press, Chicago, 1960.

Stephenson, Nathaniel W., *Texas and the Mexican War,* The Chronicles of America, Yale University Press, New Haven, 1919.

Tinkle, Lon, *13 Days to Glory—The Siege of the Alamo,* McGraw-Hill Book Co., Inc., New York, 1958.

Weigley, Russell F., *The American Way of War,* Macmillan Publishing Co., Inc., New York, 1973.

Index

142

The Author

Don Lawson has been interested in writing since he was a boy in Downers Grove, Illinois. His goal was to take him still deeper into the Midwest—to Iowa, where he attended Cornell College in Mount Vernon, and later graduate school at the prestigious University of Iowa Writers' Workshop. His first job was a writer's dream come true: he edited his own small town newspaper, the Nora Springs, Iowa *Advertiser*.

Then came World War II. The midwestern writer found himself in the thick of counterintelligence work for the Air Force in the European campaign for the next thirty-three months. Even then, he kept writing. His short story won first prize in *Story Magazine's* Armed Forces contest. Following the war, Lawson moved to Chicago to work on *Compton's Encyclopedia* as a staff writer. By the mid-sixties he had become editor-in-chief.

Busy as that job kept him, there was room for children's books. Deeply touched by his war experience, Lawson chose to write about all the other wars in American history. Had those wars affected other young men as strongly as he had been affected by World War II? Were the issues as important, the generals as heroic...and as human? Were the peace settlements as non-permanent? Such questions gave rise to Don Lawson's highly acclaimed Young People's History of America's Wars Series and eight other books for young readers.

Don Lawson, "The Dean of American Encyclopedia Editors," still lives in Chicago with his wife. He is presently editor-in-chief of the *American Educator Encyclopedia*.